YOUR Health

CONSULTING AUTHORS

Charlie Gibbons, Ed.D.
Associate Professor
Auburn University at Montgomery
Foundation, Secondary, and
   Physical Education Department
Montgomery, Alabama

Kathleen Middleton, MS, CHES
Administrator for Health and
   Prevention Program
Monterey County Office of Education
Monterey, California

Jan Marie Ozias, Ph.D., R.N.
Consultant, School Health Programs
Austin, Texas

Carl Anthony Stockton, Ph.D.
Professor and Department Chair
Department of Physical and
   Health Education
Radford University
Radford, Virginia

Harcourt Brace & Company

Orlando • Atlanta • Austin • Boston • San Francisco • Chicago • Dallas • New York • Toronto • London

http://www.hbschool.com

SENIOR EDITORIAL ADVISOR

Larry K. Olsen, Dr. P.H., CHES
Professor and Chair, Department of Health Science
Towson University
Towson, Maryland

REVIEWERS AND FIELD TEST TEACHERS

Linda Ashby
A.D. Harvey Elementary
Kingsville, Texas

Kristen Bullis
Centennial Elementary
Fargo, North Dakota

Kathy M. Burd
Polk Central Elementary
Mill Spring, North Carolina

Ada Cuadrado
PS 112 Elementary
New York, New York

James Cowden
Science Facilitator/Coordinator
Teachers Academy for
    Professional Development
Chicago Public Schools
Chicago, Illinois

Ellen Evans
Lillian Black Elementary
Spring Lake, North Carolina

Cynthia Gadson
CC Spaulding Elementary
Durham, North Carolina

Kimberly Gay
Mango Elementary
Seffner, Florida

Kenya Griffin
Sanders Elementary
Louisville, Kentucky

Sarah Grycowski
Goodland Elementary
Racine, Wisconsin

Florida H. Harding
I.P.S. 83 Elementary
Indianapolis, Indiana

Mary Jane Hollcraft
Washington Irving, School #14
Indianapolis, Indiana

Carolyn R. Jones
Johnston Elementary
Asheville, North Carolina

Rhonda Kelley
Middletown Elementary
Louisville, Kentucky

Susan Lomanto
Valley View Elementary
Longview, Texas

Karen M. Lynch
Lucy Stone Elementary
Dorchester, Massachusetts

Jane Milner
Estes Elementary
Asheville, North Carolina

Georgia Nemmers
Sycamore Trails Elementary
Bartlett, Illinois

Robin Olson
South Canyon Elementary
Rapid City, South Dakota

Beverly Sanney
Lakewood Elementary
St. Albans, West Virginia

John Torres
PS 41 Elementary
Staten Island, New York

Requests for permission to make copies of any part of the work should be mailed to the following address: School Permissions, Harcourt Brace & Company, 6277 Sea Harbor Drive, Orlando, Florida 32887-6777.

HARCOURT BRACE and Quill Design is a registered trademark of Harcourt Brace & Company.

Printed in the United States of America

ISBN 0-15-310139-3

    4 5 6 7 8 9 10 032 2000

CONSULTING HEALTH SPECIALISTS

Harriet Hylton Barr,
B.A., M.P.H., CHES
Clinical Associate Professor Emeritus
Department of Health Behavior
    and Health Education
School of Public Health
University of North Carolina
    at Chapel Hill
Durham, North Carolina

David A. Birch, Ph.D., CHES
Associate Professor
Department of Applied
    Health Science
Indiana University
Bloomington, Indiana

Glen Ceresa, D.D.S.
Clinical Instructor
Las Vegas Institute for Advanced
    Dental Studies
Las Vegas, Nevada

Michael J. Cleary, Ed.D., CHES
Professor
Department of Allied Health
Slippery Rock University
Slippery Rock, Pennsylvania

Lisa C. Cohn, M.M.Sc., M.Ed., R.D.
Nutrition Educator and
    Research Consultant
New York, New York

Mary Steckiewicz Garzino, M.Ed.
Director, Nutrition Education
National Dairy Council
Chicago, Illinois

Mark L. Giese, Ed.D., FACSM
Professor
Northeastern Oklahoma
    State University
Tahlequah, Oklahoma

Michael J. Hammes, Ph.D.
Associate Professor
University of New Mexico
Albuquerque, New Mexico

Betty M. Hubbard, Ed.D., CHES
Professor of Health Education
Department of Health Sciences
University of Central Arkansas
Conway, Arkansas

Rama K. Khalsa, Ph.D.
Director of Mental Health
Santa Cruz County
Soquel, California

Darrel Lang, Ed.D.
Health and Physical
    Education Consultant
Kansas State Department
    of Education
Emporia, Kansas

Gerald J. Maburn
National Vice President for Planning
    and Evaluation
American Cancer Society
Atlanta, Georgia

Cheryl Miller-Haymowicz,
B.S., CHES
Health Educator
Salem-Keizer Public Schools
Salem, Oregon

John A. Morris, M.S.W.
Professor of Neuropsychiatry
    and Behavioral Science
University of South Carolina
    School of Medicine
Director of Interdisciplinary Affairs
South Carolina Department
    of Mental Health
Columbia, South Carolina

Patricia Poindexter, M.P.H., CHES
Health Education Specialist
Tucker, Georgia

Janine Robinette
Health Program Administrator
Monterey, California

Spencer Sartorius, M.S.
Administrator
Health Enhancement and
    Safety Division
Montana Office of
    Public Instruction
Helena, Montana

Jeanne Marie Scott, M.D.
Staff Physician
San Jose State University
San Jose, California

David A. Sleet, Ph.D.
Centers for Disease Control
    and Prevention
Atlanta, Georgia

Becky J. Smith,
Ph.D., CHES
Reston, Virginia

Howard Taras, M.D.
Associate Professor
(Specialist in Medical Consultation
    to Schools)
University of California at
    San Diego
San Diego, California

Pamela M. Tollefsen, R.N., M.Ed.
Program Supervisor, Health
    Education
Office of Superintendent of Public
    Instruction
State of Washington
Olympia, Washington

Mae Waters, Ph.D., CHES
Executive Director of Comprehensive
    Health Training
Florida State University
Tallahassee, Florida

Contents

Chapter 1 — Me and My Feelings 14

Emotional, Intellectual, and Social Health

The Amazing Human Body

*Getting rest,
eating right, and
staying active are
the first steps to
a healthful life.*

1

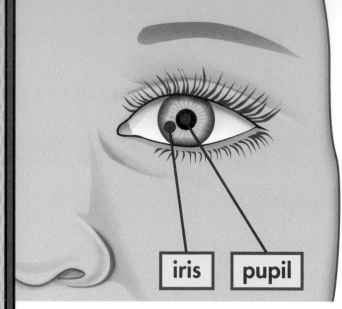

Outside of Eye

Caring for Your Eyes and Ears

- Some bright light can hurt your eyes. Never look at the sun or at very bright lights.
- Never put an object in your ear.

Eyes

When you look at your eyes, you can see a white part, a colored part, and a dark center. The colored part is the iris. The dark center is the pupil.

Inside of Eye

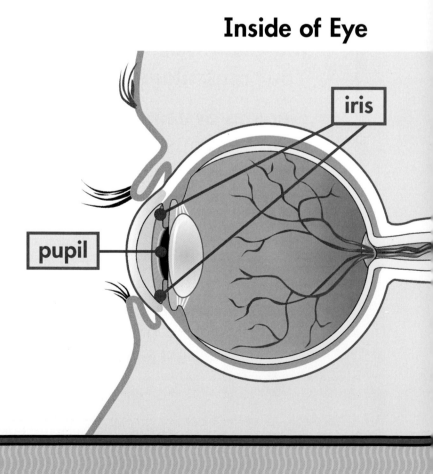

Ear

Your ears let you hear. Most of each ear is inside your head.

inner ear   middle ear   outer ear

eardrum

Inside of Ear   **Outside of Ear**

ACTIVITIES

1. The iris of the eye may be different colors. Look at the eyes of your classmates. How many colors do you see?

2. Ask a classmate to stand across the classroom from you. Have him or her say your name in a normal voice. Now put a hand behind each ear and have him or her say your name again in the same voice. Which time sounded louder?

The Skeletal System

Inside your body are hard, strong bones. They make up your skeleton. Your skeleton holds you up.

Caring for Your Skeletal System

Protect your head. Wear a helmet when you ride your bike.

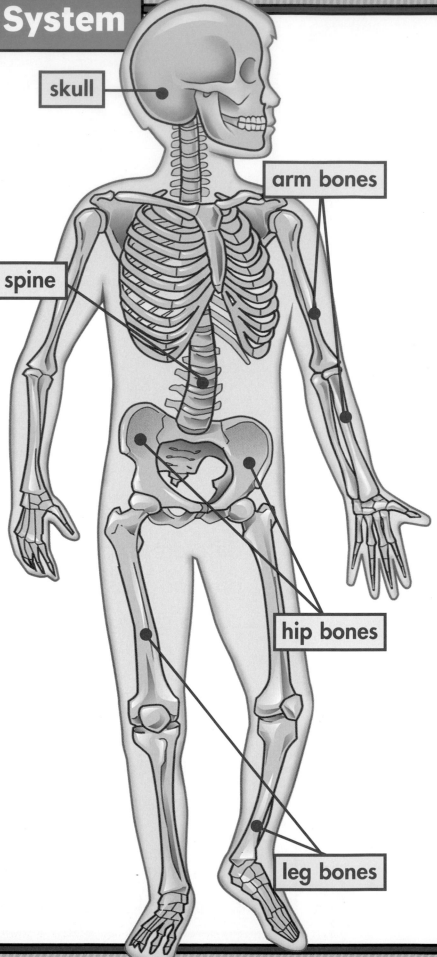

skull

arm bones

spine

hip bones

leg bones

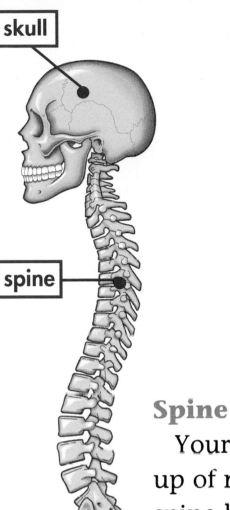

skull

spine

Skull

The bones in your head are called your skull. Your skull protects your brain.

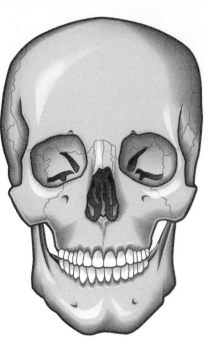

Spine

Your spine, or backbone, is made up of many small bones. Your spine helps you stand up straight.

ACTIVITIES

1. Look at a bike helmet. How is it like your skull?

2. Your foot is about the same length as your arm between your hand and your elbow. Put your foot on your arm and check it out!

The Digestive System

Your digestive system helps your body get energy from the food you eat.

Caring for Your Digestive System

- Brush and floss your teeth every day.

- Don't eat right before you exercise. Your body needs energy to digest food.

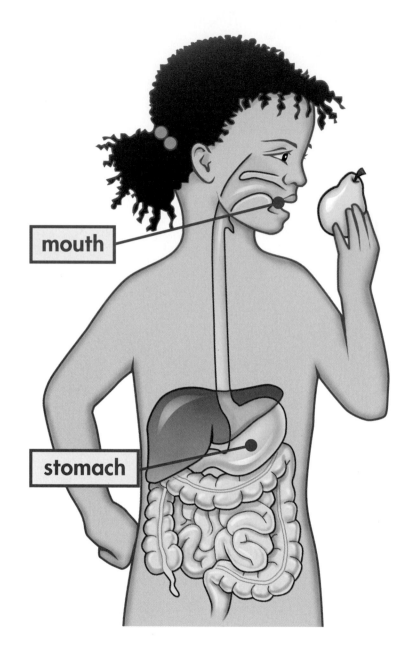

mouth

stomach

Teeth

Some of your teeth tear food and some grind it into small parts.

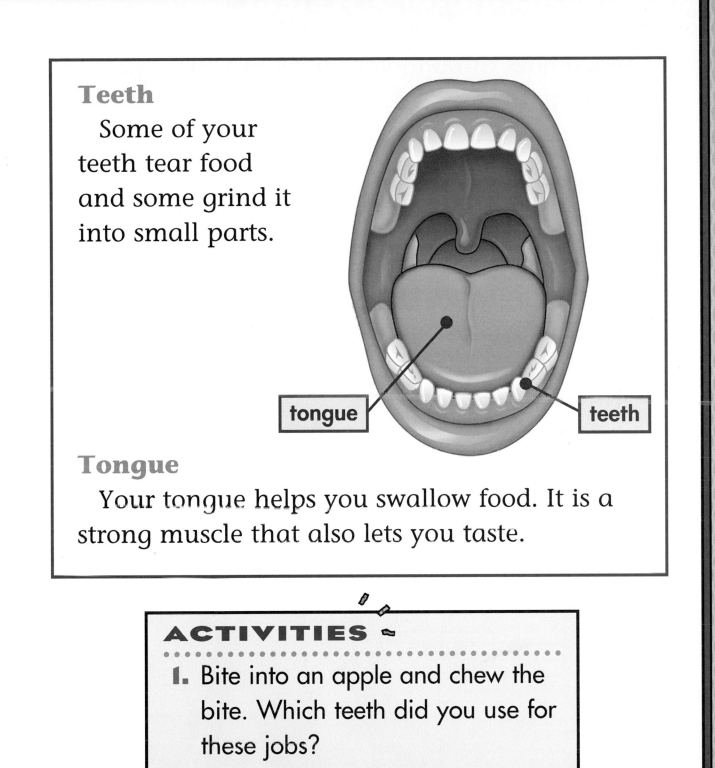

tongue

teeth

Tongue

Your tongue helps you swallow food. It is a strong muscle that also lets you taste.

ACTIVITIES

1. Bite into an apple and chew the bite. Which teeth did you use for these jobs?

2. Lick a salty pretzel and a lollipop. Which one can you taste better with just the tip of your tongue?

The Circulatory System

Blood goes through your body in your circulatory system. Your heart pumps the blood. Your blood vessels carry the blood.

Caring for Your Circulatory System

- Exercise every day to keep your heart strong.
- Keep germs out of your blood. Wash cuts with soap and water. Never touch someone else's blood.

blood vessels

heart

Heart

Your heartbeat is the sound of your heart pumping. Your heart is about the same size as a fist.

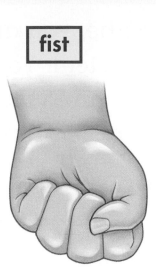

fist

blood vessels

heart

Blood Vessels

Blood vessels are tubes that carry blood through your body.

ACTIVITIES

1. Ask an adult to blow up a hot-dog shaped balloon so that it is not quite full. Squeeze one end. What happens?

2. Put your ear to the middle of a classmate's chest and listen to the heartbeat. Then listen again through a paper cup with the bottom torn out. Which way of listening works better?

The Respiratory System

When you breathe, you are using your respiratory system. Your mouth, your nose, and your lungs are parts of your respiratory system.

Caring for Your Respiratory System

- Never put anything in your nose.
- Exercise makes you breathe harder and is good for your lungs.

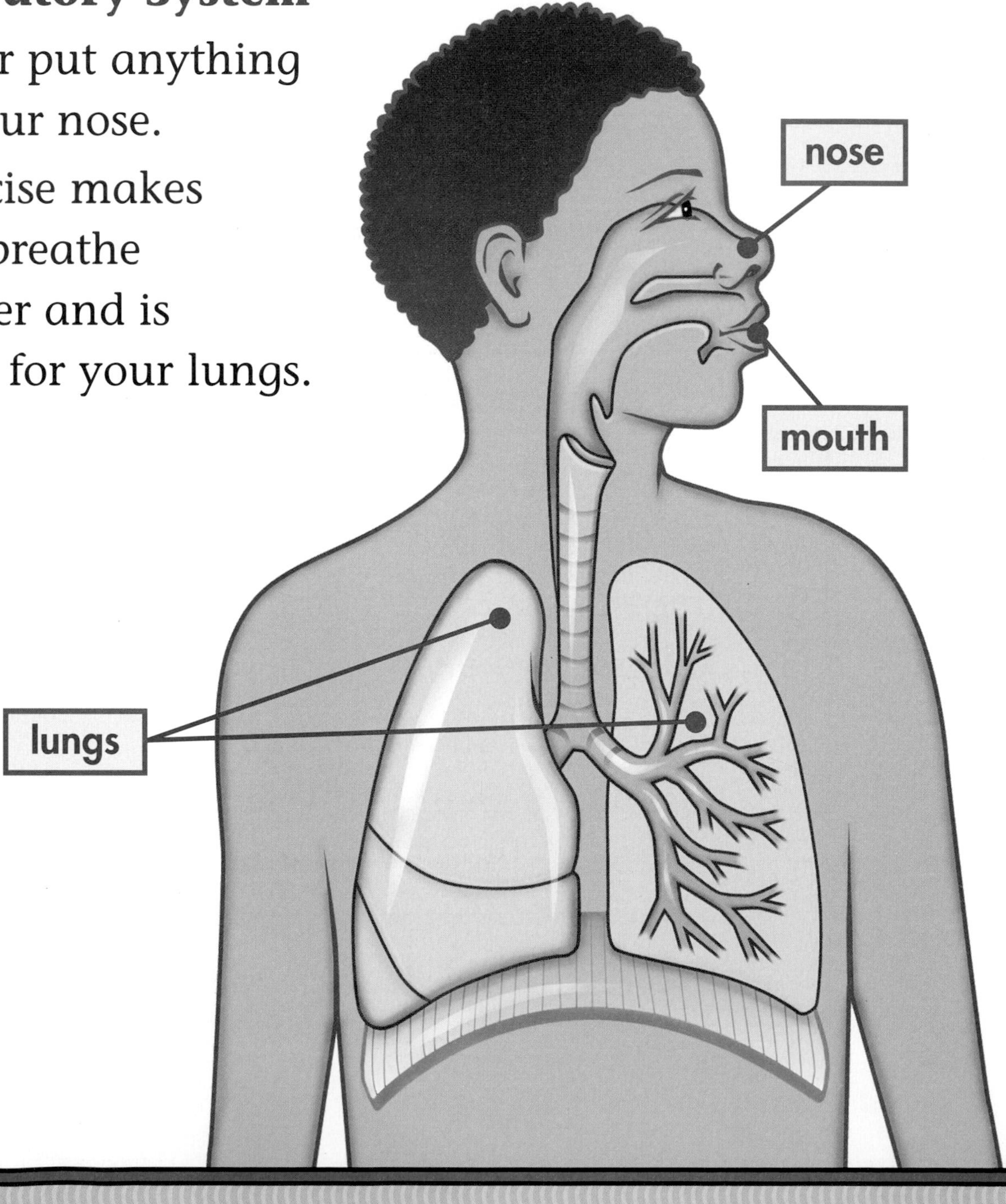

nose

mouth

lungs

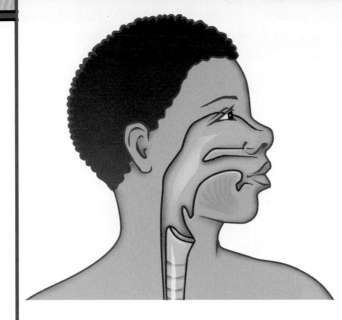

Mouth and Nose

Air goes in and out of your body through your mouth and nose.

Lungs

You have two lungs in your chest. When you breathe in, your lungs fill with air. When you breathe out, air leaves your lungs.

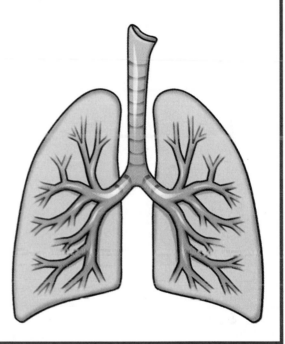

ACTIVITIES

1. Watch your chest and stomach muscles as you take a breath and let it out. Describe what happens.

2. Count how many breaths you take in one minute.

The Muscular System

The muscles in your body help you move.

Caring for Your Muscular System

Warm up your muscles before you play or exercise.

ACTIVITY

Hold your arm straight out from your body and lift it over your head. Then try it again with a book in your hand. How do the muscles in your arm feel?

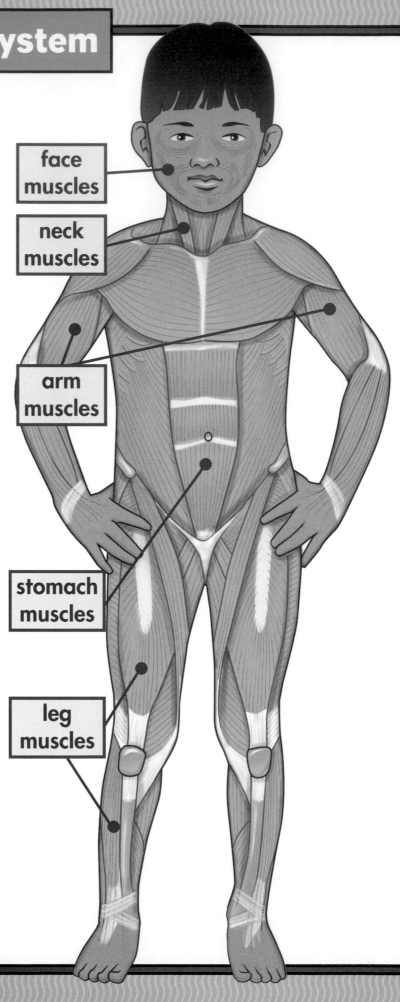

face muscles

neck muscles

arm muscles

stomach muscles

leg muscles

The Nervous System

brain

nerves

Your nervous system keeps your body working and tells you about things around you. Your brain is part of your nervous system.

Caring for Your Nervous System

Get plenty of sleep. Sleeping lets your brain rest.

ACTIVITY

Clap your hands in front of a classmate's face. What happens to his or her eyes?

Me and My Feelings

Project

Happy Days
Draw a picture of
a time when you
were very happy.
Tell why you
were happy.

For more things to do,
visit the Internet.
http://www.hbschool.com

What makes me special?

You are special. **Special** is what makes you different from others.

No one looks just like you. No one acts just like you.

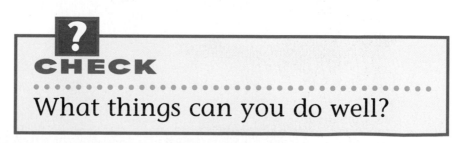

You can do some things very well.
What things are these children
doing that make them special?

?

CHECK
· ·
What things can you do well?

What are feelings?

You have feelings. Everyone has feelings. **Feelings** are what you feel inside when you are happy, sad, afraid, or excited.

Sometimes you like your feelings. Sometimes you do not like them. It is OK to have many kinds of feelings.

What things might make someone feel happy?

What things might make someone feel sad?

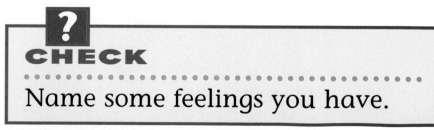

? CHECK

Name some feelings you have.

How can I show my feelings?

You can use words to tell how you feel. Or you can show your feelings.

There are many ways to show how you feel.

Sometimes you laugh. Sometimes you cry. Sometimes you jump up and down.

What things do you do to show that you are happy or excited?

?
CHECK
Look at the pictures. What feelings are the children showing?

21

What should I do when I feel angry?

Everyone feels **angry** sometimes. It is OK to feel angry. It is not OK to hurt another person when you are angry.

Talking might help you feel better. Playing might help you feel better.

? CHECK

Use the pictures to tell a story. Tell what the girl does when she feels angry.

MANAGE STRESS

Molly is going to sleep over at Hannah's house. It is her first time sleeping away from her family. Molly is excited, but she is also worried. Molly feels **stress**. What should Molly do?

Learn This Skill

1. Know what stress feels like.

Molly's heart beats fast. She is not sure she is ready to sleep away from home.

2. Think about ways to handle stress.

Don't worry. You can call us if you need us.

Molly could talk with her parents about how she feels.

3. Think about one step at a time.

Molly thinks about how nice Hannah is. She thinks about having fun with Hannah and her family.

4. Learn ways to relax.

Molly takes a deep breath. She says to herself, "I know I will have fun. I can come home if I need to."

Practice This Skill

Use the steps to help you solve this problem.

You will be riding the school bus for the first time tomorrow. You feel stress. What can you do to feel better?

5

How can I respect others?

It is fun to play and study with others. Treating others nicely is called **respect**. You can get along with others better if you respect them.

Helping others shows respect.
Being kind shows respect.

If you respect others, you are not mean to them. You do not say or do unkind things.

? CHECK

Tell why you think respect helps people get along better.

How can I be a friend?

Friends are fun. You can talk to **friends**. You can play with them. You can share with them. Friends are kind to each other.

To have a friend, be a friend!

There are many ways to make friends. Making new friends is fun!

? CHECK

Name three ways you can be a good friend.

Review

Use Health Words

special **feelings** **angry**
stress **respect** **friends**

Finish the sentences.

1. Happiness, sadness, and anger are kinds of ___.

2. The things you can do well make you ___.

3. People you have fun with are ___.

4. It is not OK to hurt another person when you are ___.

5. Helping others is a way to show ___.

6. When you are excited, afraid, or worried, you can do things to manage your ___.

Use Health Ideas

Tell how the children in the pictures are feeling.

7.  8. 9.

Use Life Skills

Answer the question.

10. Toby is new in class. He feels shy and afraid. Toby feels stress. Tell what Toby could do to feel better.

Activities

- **On Your Own** Draw a picture that shows one way you are special.

- **With a Partner** Take turns acting out different feelings. Guess what feeling your partner is acting out.

- **At Home** Have a family member help you make a list of things to do when you feel angry or afraid.

My Senses Help Me Grow

Project

Watch Me Grow!
Plant a seed, or
take care of a
small plant.
Watch how your
plant grows. Tell
what happens.

For more things to do,
visit the Internet.
http://www.hbschool.com

What are living things?

Plants, animals, and people are living things. All **living** things are alive. They use food to grow.

Living things come from other living things. You are a living thing.

Rocks, water, and air are some things that are not alive. Things that are not alive are called **nonliving** things. They do not need food.

? CHECK

Name three living things and three nonliving things.

What are my senses?

You use your senses every day. People have five senses. The **senses** are sight, hearing, smell, taste, and touch. You use a different part of your body for each sense.

see

hear

touch

smell

taste

Think about how you use your
senses every day. Name five ways
you use your senses.

?
CHECK
Point to the parts of your body
where your senses are.

Why are my senses important?

Your senses help you find out about the world. They help you enjoy things. Your senses help you learn things.

See!
Hear!
Smell!
Taste!
Touch!

How are these children using
their senses?

? CHECK

How do your senses help you?

39

4

How will I grow?

Once you were a baby. Now you are a child. One day you will become an adult.

You are growing!

Becoming bigger and taller means you are **growing**. Your muscles and bones are growing. You weigh more.

Everybody grows.

?

CHECK

Name one way you are growing.

How do people in families help one another?

You have a family. Your **family** is people such as a mom, a dad, a sister, and a brother. Every family is different.

Family members show love for other family members. The special feeling you have for your family is called **love**. People in families help one another by showing love and kindness.

? CHECK

How can you help someone in your family?

6

Why should I be polite?

You show respect for others when you are polite. Being **polite** means treating others nicely. When you are polite, you think about what others need.

You know that it is good to be polite and show respect at school. But you need to be polite at home, too.

Families get along best when everyone is polite and shows respect.

? CHECK

Name two ways you can be polite to your family.

RESOLVE CONFLICTS
at Home

When people have a **conflict**, they do not agree. People in families sometimes have conflicts. How can family members get along better?

Learn This Skill

1. Stop.

Bill and Tom each want to take the same video game to a friend's home. They need to stop fighting.

2. Agree that there is a problem.

Both boys want to play. If one takes the game away, the other will not be able to play.

3. Think of ways to work together.

The boys think of different ideas.

4. Make the best choice.

All the boys play together. They take turns. They have fun.

Practice This Skill

Use the steps to help you solve this problem.

Doris has a new skateboard. Her brother has borrowed it without asking. Doris is angry. How can Doris and her brother resolve their conflict?

What do families do together?

You can do many things with your family. You can talk or eat a meal together. You can share. You might play games.

You can also help around the house. A family can work together to get things done.

? CHECK

What are some things you do with your family?

Use Health Words

living   nonliving   senses   growing
family   love   polite

Finish the sentences.

1. Things that are not alive are ___.

2. Getting bigger means you are ___.

3. One of your ___ is used for seeing.

4. Plants, people, and animals are ___ things.

5. A parent is a member of a ___.

6. Treating others nicely is being ___.

7. People in families show ___ for one another.

Use Health Ideas

Draw the body part or write its name.

8. What do you use to smell?

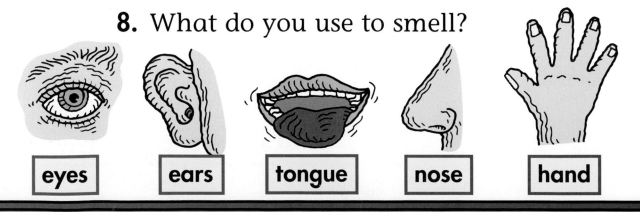

eyes   ears   tongue   nose   hand

9. What do you use to hear?

10. What do you use to taste?

Use Life Skills

Use the picture.
Answer the question.

11. Andrew and Jane both want to ride. Tell a way they can work out their conflict.

Activities

- **On Your Own** Make a collage that shows living things.

- **At Home** List three ways you can help your family. Make coupons to give to family members.

My Teeth

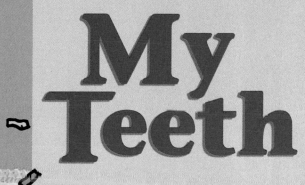

Smile Make a poster to remind you to take care of your teeth. On your poster, draw a picture of yourself with a big smile.

For more things to do, visit the Internet.
http://www.hbschool.com

What do teeth do?

You use your teeth when you eat. Your teeth are not all the same. You use different teeth for different things.

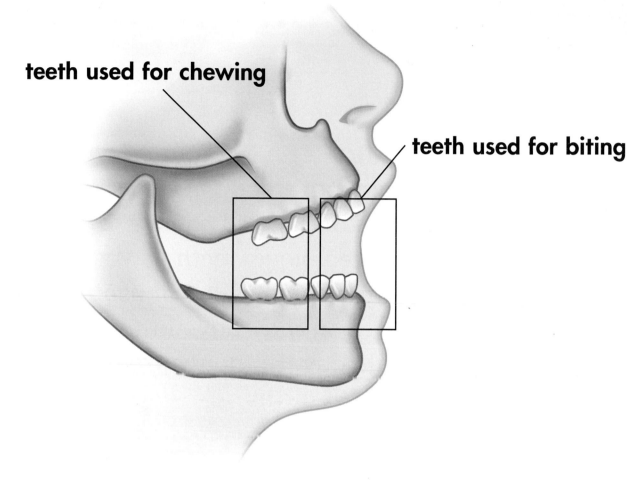

teeth used for chewing

teeth used for biting

Your front teeth are sharp. They help you bite into food. Your back teeth are wide. They help you chew food so you can swallow it easily.

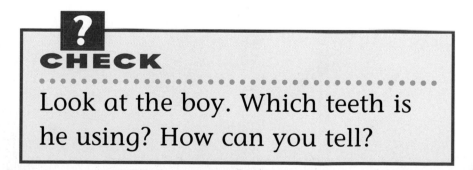

? CHECK

Look at the boy. Which teeth is he using? How can you tell?

Why do I lose teeth?

Your first teeth are your baby teeth. They grow in when you are small. They are also called **primary teeth**.

You need bigger teeth as you grow. Soon your baby teeth will begin to fall out. You may have lost some teeth already. Do not worry. Other teeth will grow in.

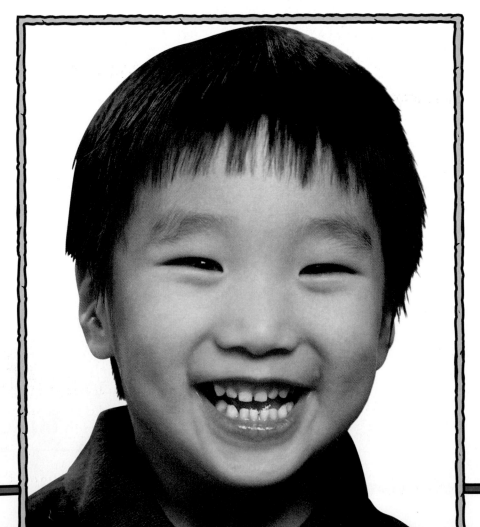

The new teeth are called **permanent teeth**. Take good care of them. You should try to keep your permanent teeth for the rest of your life.

? CHECK

Why do you lose your baby teeth?

How should I brush my teeth?

Brush your teeth every day. Brush them when you get up in the morning. Brush them before you go to bed. Try to brush your teeth after you eat.

Brushing helps keep your teeth clean and healthy.

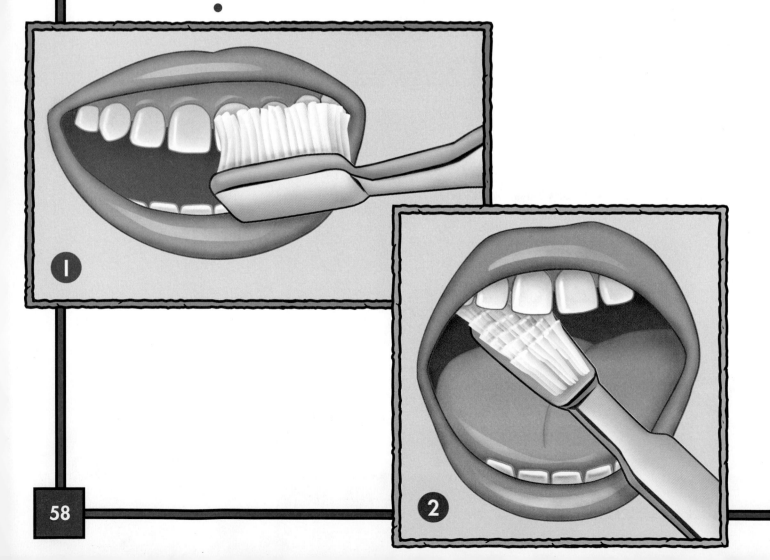

Use a toothbrush that is the right size for you. Use toothpaste and water. The pictures show how to brush your teeth. Brush the outsides. Brush the insides. Then brush the tops.

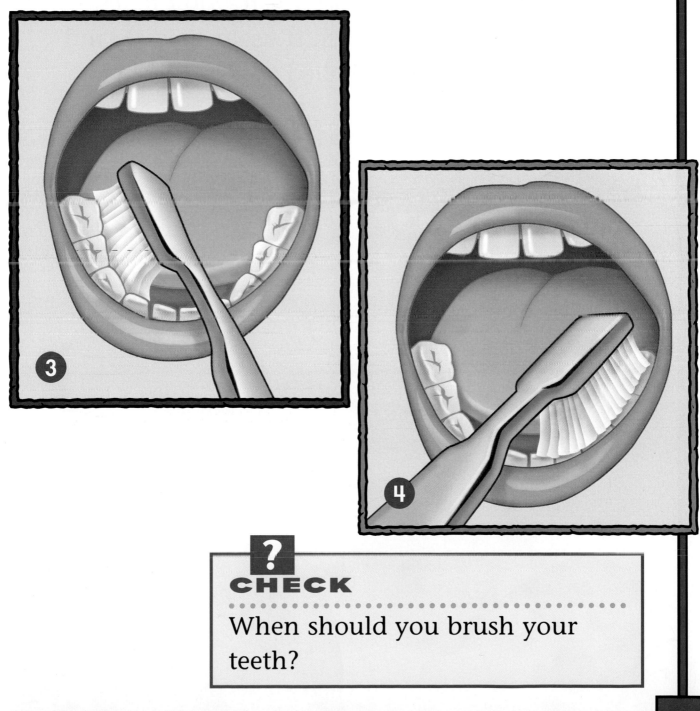

?

CHECK

When should you brush your teeth?

How should I floss my teeth?

You need to clean between your teeth. A toothbrush won't reach there. You must use a special kind of thread called **floss**.

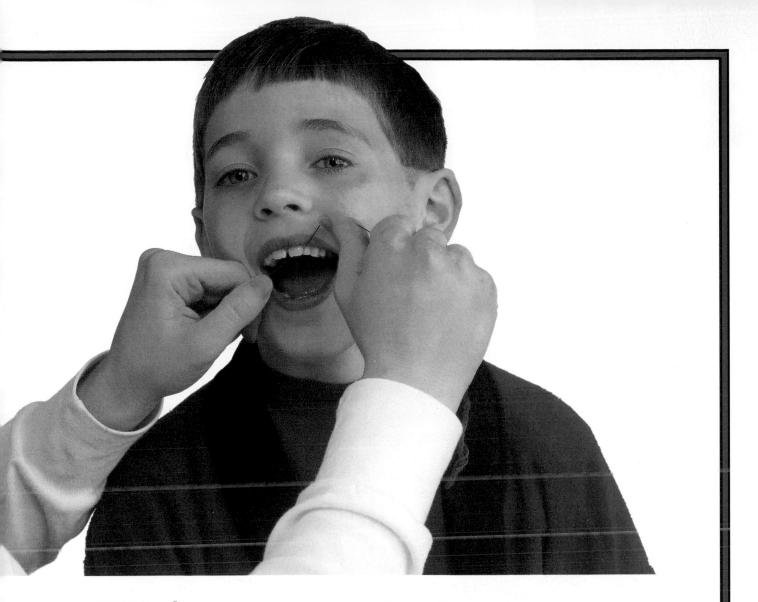

Clean between your teeth to keep them healthy. You should floss once a day. The best time to floss is before you go to bed.

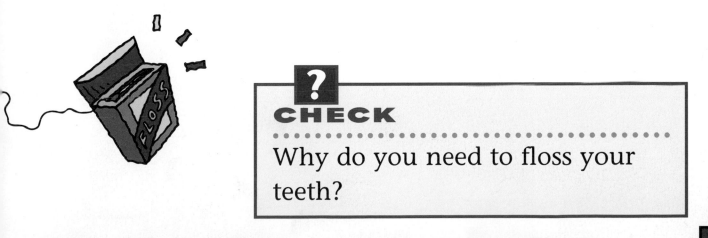

? CHECK

Why do you need to floss your teeth?

How can I keep my teeth safe?

You need your teeth to eat. Your teeth help you bite into food. They help you break food into tiny pieces.

You can harm your teeth by doing the wrong things. Use your teeth only for eating. Take good care of your teeth.

? CHECK

Draw a child doing something that can harm teeth. Put an X across the picture.

MAKE DECISIONS
About Caring for Your Teeth

You can make decisions that will help keep your teeth healthy. Help Bo make a healthful decision about his teeth.

Learn This Skill

1. Think before you choose.

Bo wants to open the bag. How can he do it?

2. Imagine what could happen with each choice.

Using his teeth could make Bo's teeth hurt. Using scissors will not hurt at all.

3. Make the best choice.

Bo decides to use scissors to open the bag.

4. Think about what happened.

Bo is happy that he did not hurt his teeth.

Practice This Skill

Use the steps to help you solve this problem.

Kai is tired. She knows she should brush her teeth before bed. She looks at her teeth in the mirror. They look clean to her. What should Kai do?

What happens when I visit the dentist?

People called **dentists** know all about teeth. They help you take good care of your teeth.

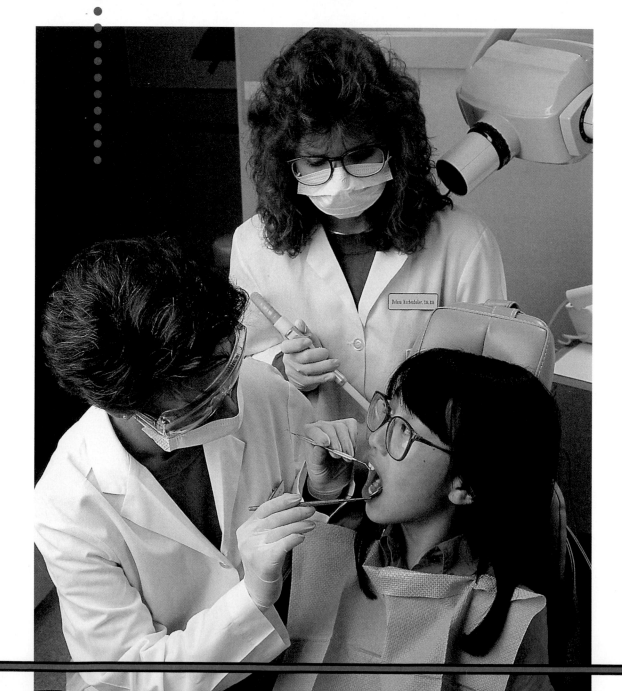

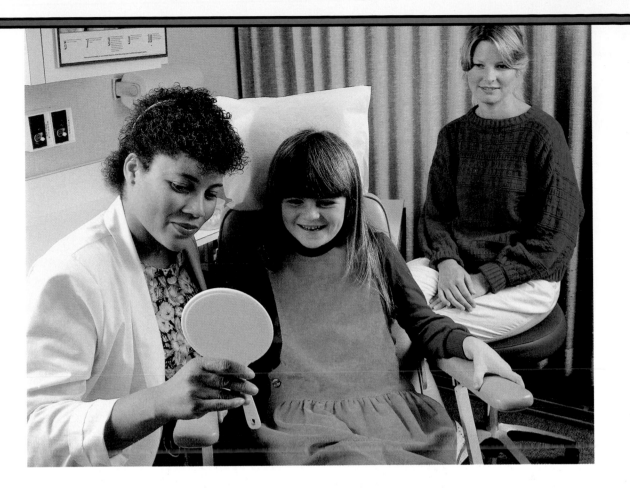

Dentists check for problems. Do your teeth work together? Are they clean? Do they have any holes? Dentists know how to fix tooth problems.

Sometimes a dentist cleans your teeth. Often a **dental hygienist** cleans them instead.

?

CHECK

How can a dentist and a dental hygienist help you?

Use Health Words

permanent teeth **floss**

dental hygienist **primary teeth**

Finish the sentences.

1. You use ___ to clean between your teeth.

2. After you lose your baby teeth, you get your ___.

3. A ___ often cleans your teeth.

4. Baby teeth are also called ___.

Use Health Ideas

Write the name.

5. Which teeth are used for chewing?

6. Which teeth are used for biting?

Write the correct answer.

outsides   **insides**   **tops**

7. Brush the ___ of your teeth first.

8. Brush the ___ of your teeth second.

9. Brush the ___ of your teeth last.

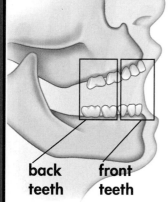

back teeth   front teeth

Use Life Skills

Answer the questions.

10. What four steps can you use to help make a good choice?

11. You are staying overnight at your friend's house. You forgot your toothbrush. What will you choose to do?

Activities

- **With a Partner** Pretend you each have a toothbrush. Practice the right way to brush your teeth. Have your partner check how you do.

- **At Home** Learn how to floss. Ask an adult for help.

- **On Your Own** Draw a picture of yourself at the dentist's office. Show the dentist or the dental hygienist.

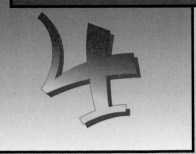

Taking Care of My Body

A Healthy Day

Make a list of everything you do in one day. Circle the things that will help you stay healthy.

For more things to do, visit the Internet.
http://www.hbschool.com

Why should I keep clean?

Staying clean helps you stay healthy. Soap and water kill **germs** that can make you ill.

Germs are too tiny to see. Washing your hands and wearing clean clothes are good ways to fight germs.

Wash your hands for as long as it takes to say your ABCs!

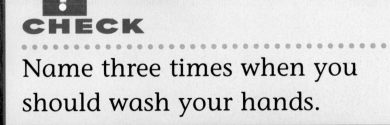

? CHECK

Name three times when you should wash your hands.

How can I keep my skin healthy?

Staying clean is one way to keep your skin healthy. Another good way is to protect your skin from sunburn. **Sunburn** is a burning of the skin caused by the sun's rays.

You can get a sunburn anytime you go outside during the day. You can even get a sunburn on a cloudy day!

Protect your skin by wearing sunscreen. **Sunscreen** keeps the sun's rays from burning your skin.

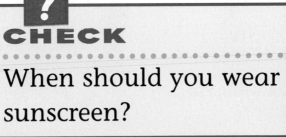

?

CHECK

When should you wear sunscreen?

What is good posture?

Your **posture** is the way you hold your body when you stand, sit, or move. Good posture helps you look your best. It makes it easier for you to breathe. Good posture helps your body grow.

Good posture for sitting means your head is up. Your shoulders are back. Your feet are flat on the floor.

Good posture for standing or walking means your back is straight, your head is up, and your shoulders are back.

? CHECK

How does having good posture help you?

Why should I exercise?

Run! Jump! Swim! It is fun to exercise. **Exercise** is active use of your body.

Exercise helps keep your heart and lungs healthy. It helps you fight off germs. You feel better when you exercise.

Exercise is more fun when you choose an activity you like. Look at how these children are exercising. Think of three ways you exercise every day.

?
CHECK

Name two ways that exercise helps you.

MANAGE STRESS
with Exercise

Chen's mother is away on a business trip. Chen is afraid his father will forget to pick him up after school. How can Chen manage his stress?

Learn This Skill

1. Know what stress feels like.

Chen's heart is beating fast. His stomach hurts when he thinks about being alone.

2. Think about ways to handle stress.

Chen thinks about how he can pass the time until his father comes.

3. Take one step at a time.

Chen decides to manage his stress by exercising with his friends.

4. Learn ways to relax.

Chen! I'm here!

Hi, Dad! You're early!

Chen was having such a good time that he forgot about his fear.

Practice This Skill

Use the steps to help you solve this problem.

It is two hours until Paula's birthday party. All her friends will be there. Paula is so excited! She feels she can't wait for the party. What can Paula do to help herself be calm?

How can I exercise safely?

Exercise is fun, but you need to exercise safely. Here are four ways to stay safe while you exercise.

Stretch your muscles before and after you exercise.

Drink lots of water because you lose water when you exercise.

Stop to rest when you feel tired or too hot.

Choose the right activity for the weather.

Don't run hard when it's very hot! Don't go hiking in a snowstorm!

?

CHECK

Why should you drink water when you exercise?

Why do I need sleep?

Your body needs sleep to stay healthy. While you sleep, your bones and muscles grow. Your body rests and fights germs while you are sleeping.

When you get enough sleep, you have the strength you need to run and play. Learning is easier when you are rested.

85

CHECK

What do you think happens when you don't get enough sleep?

Review

CHAPTER 4

Use Health Words

germs	sunburn	sunscreen
posture	exercise	stretch

Finish the sentences.

1. Keep your skin healthy by not getting a ___.

2. Soap kills ___ that can make you ill.

3. Put on ___ to keep the sun's rays from burning your skin.

4. Running, jumping, and swimming are ways to ___.

5. Good ___ helps you breathe easier.

6. Before and after exercising, be sure to ___ your muscles.

Use Health Ideas

Answer the questions.

7. Why should you wear sunscreen on a cloudy day?

8. Name two ways that getting enough sleep helps your body.

Use the picture to answer the question.

9. What would you tell these children to do so they will have good posture?

Use Life Skills

Answer the question.

10. How can exercise help you manage stress?

Activities

- **On Your Own** Make a poster showing ways to stay healthy.
- **With a Team** Have a relay race. Remember to stretch your muscles before and after you run.

Wonderful Food

Go Shopping

Pretend you are shopping at a farmers' market. Choose three foods to share with the class. Which food do you think is most healthful? Tell why.

For more things to do, visit the Internet.
http://www.hbschool.com

1

Why do I need food?

Food helps your body grow and stay healthy. Food also gives you energy. **Energy** is the power your body needs to do things.

Look at how these children are using energy. How do you use energy each day? Think of three ways.

Why does your body need food?

What groups of food do I need?

fats, sweets

milk, yogurt, cheese

vegetables

bread, cereal, rice, pasta

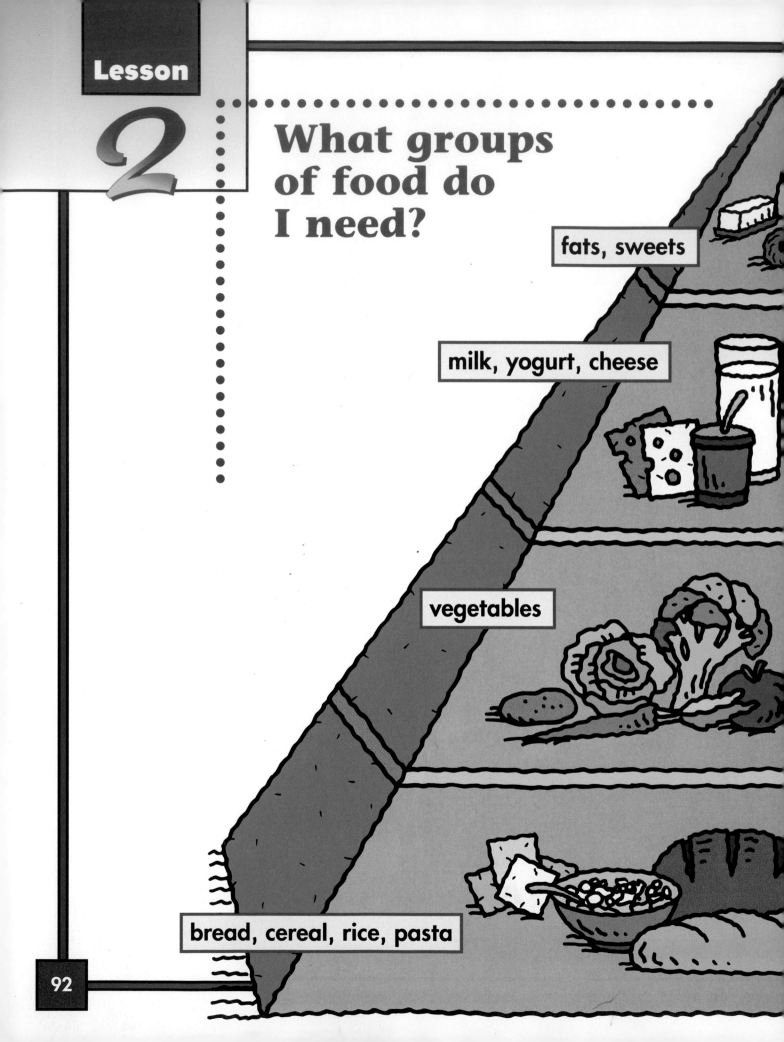

This **Food Guide Pyramid** helps people choose what to eat. You need to eat food from all the groups in the Food Guide Pyramid.

Look at the pyramid. The food group at the bottom is the largest. Eat many foods from this group.

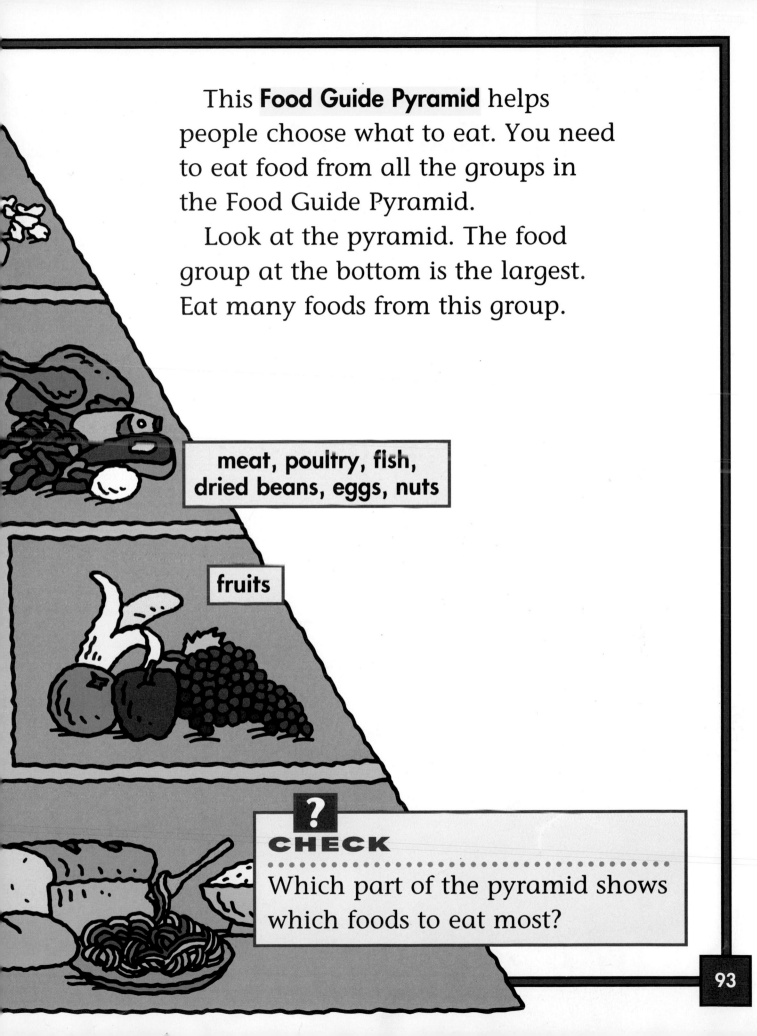

meat, poultry, fish, dried beans, eggs, nuts

fruits

?

CHECK

Which part of the pyramid shows which foods to eat most?

93

What foods are in each food group?

Look at the foods. What foods are in each food group?

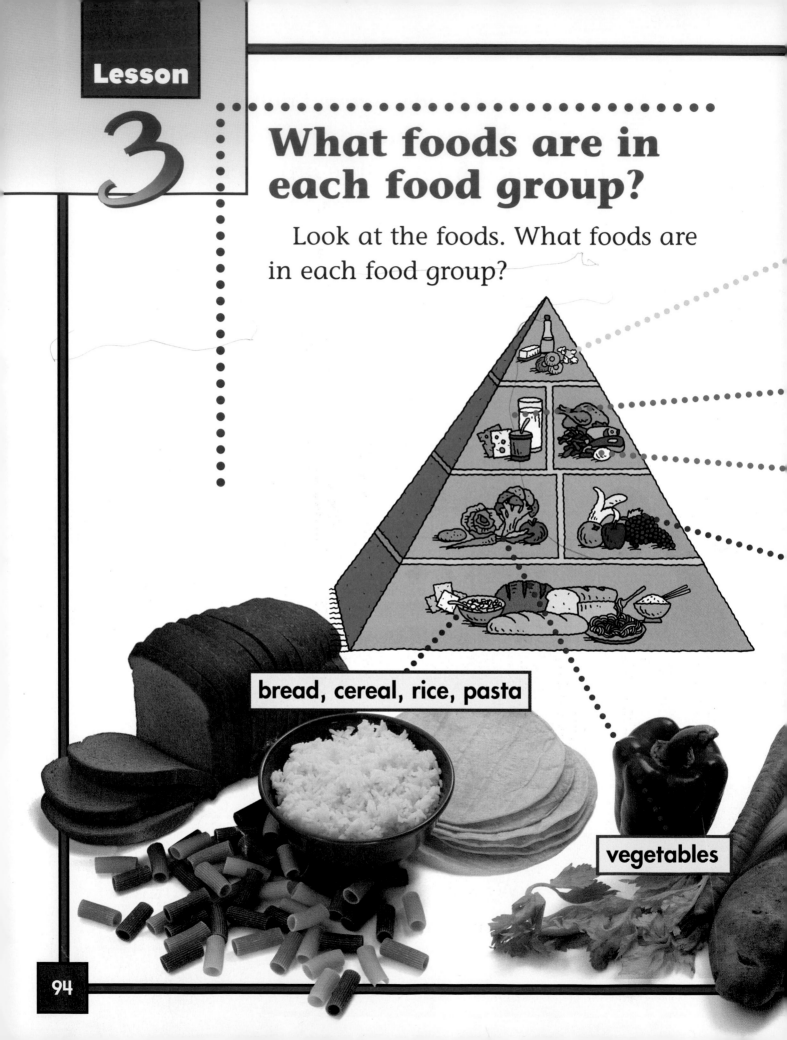

bread, cereal, rice, pasta

vegetables

fats, sweets

milk, yogurt, cheese

meat, poultry, fish,
dried beans, eggs, nuts

fruits

? CHECK

Name a food you eat from each food group.

4

Why should I try new foods?

It takes many kinds of foods to help your body grow and stay healthy. No one food can give you all the energy you need.

Trying new foods can be fun. You may even find a new food you really like. If you do not try, you will never know.

These children are using their
five **senses** to learn about new foods.
Taste is one sense. What other senses
are the children using? What are
they learning?

CHECK

Tell how you can use taste,
sight, hearing, smell, and touch
to learn about new foods.

Why should I eat meals?

Eating a meal is a good way to get foods from many food groups. **Breakfast**, **lunch**, and **dinner** are three meals that many people eat every day.

A good breakfast gives you energy to start your day. Eating lunch and dinner helps your body get the energy it needs all day long.

Breakfast

Lunch

Dinner

? CHECK

Tell which food groups the foods in these meals belong to.

MAKE DECISIONS
About Food

Making good choices about food will help keep you healthy. How can you choose foods that will give you the energy you need?

Learn This Skill

1. Think before you choose.

Al wants to choose a breakfast food. It must give his body energy for his soccer game.

2. Imagine what could happen with each choice.

SCORE!

YAWN!

Choosing cereal will give Al's body energy. Sweets may leave Al tired during the game.

3. Make the best choice.

Al chooses cereal, lowfat milk, fruit, and toast.

4. Think about what happened.

Go Al!

Al had energy to play and have fun.

Practice This Skill

Use the steps to help you solve this problem.

You want lunch. You can have a cheese sandwich, an apple, and milk. Or you can have a hot dog, chips, and a soda. Which lunch will you choose?

What makes a healthful snack?

Sometimes you feel hungry between meals. Then you should eat a **snack**. Snacks give you extra energy for work and play.

Choose snacks from different food groups. Some snack foods come from the top of the Food Guide Pyramid. Eat only small amounts of these snacks.

Watch out for fat, salt, and sugar!

? CHECK

Look at the pictures. Choose two healthful snacks you like.

What are food ads?

An **ad** is a message that tries to get you to buy something. You see many ads for snacks on TV.

An ad may use a catchy tune or show someone famous. It may even offer you a free surprise.

Some ads make snack foods seem healthful. But they are really full of sugar, fat, or salt.

Look at the ad. How does it try to get you to buy Supersweets? What else do you need to know about Supersweets?

?
CHECK

What should you watch and listen for in food ads?

Review

Use Health Words

energy   Food Guide Pyramid
senses   breakfast, lunch, and dinner
snack   ad

Finish the sentences.

1. You use your ___ of sight and taste to learn about new foods.

2. Food gives your body ___.

3. The ___ helps you choose what to eat each day.

4. You should eat ___ every day.

5. A food ___ on TV may not always tell you what you need to know.

6. If you get hungry between meals, eat a healthful ___.

Use Health Ideas

Answer the questions.

7. What should you avoid to have a healthful snack?

8. Why should you try new foods?

Use Life Skills

Use the pictures to help you answer
the questions.

9. Which is the healthful meal?
   Tell why.

10. Tell four steps that can help you
    make your choice.

Activities

- **On Your Own**
  Paste pictures of a
  healthful meal on
  a paper plate.

- **With a Team**
  Make up an ad for
  a favorite food.

Fruit is good for Snacks.

Staying Well

Project

A Wellness Book
Make a book of
ideas for staying
healthy and
fighting germs.

For more things to do,
visit the Internet.
http://www.hbschool.com

How can I tell if I am ill?

When you are **ill**, you are not healthy. Parts of your body may hurt. Your head or your stomach may ache. You may have a fever that makes your skin feel hot.

Tell your teacher if you feel ill at school. Tell your family if you feel ill at home. Try to tell or show what hurts.

?
CHECK
Name two changes in your body that help you know you are ill.

COMMUNICATE
When You Are Ill

When you talk to someone, you **communicate**. The person you are talking to understands you. It is important to communicate when you do not feel well.

Cal needs help. He does not feel well.

Learn This Skill

1. Decide whom to talk to.

Cal wakes up. He feels ill. He knows he can tell his parents that he does not feel well.

2. Say what you need to say.

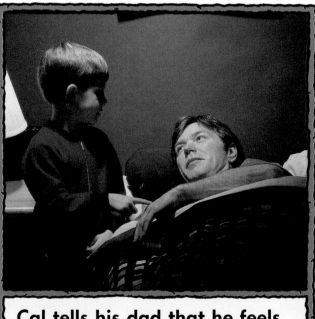

Cal tells his dad that he feels very hot. He also says his throat hurts.

3. Listen.

Cal's dad says Cal's temperature is high. He says Cal has a fever and his throat is red.

4. Get information.

Cal asks what the medicine will do. His dad says it will help Cal's fever.

Practice This Skill

Use the steps to help you solve this problem.

Jenny feels ill at school. Her stomach hurts. Whom should she tell? What should she tell that person?

How is illness spread?

You know that germs can cause disease. **Disease** is another name for illness. Illness is spread when germs are spread.

Sneezing and coughing can spread germs. Blowing your nose can also spread germs. Touching your mouth, eyes, or nose with unwashed hands can lead to disease.

AH-CHOO!

You can do things to stop the spread of germs. Stopping germs is a way to fight disease.

Sharing is good, but don't share germs!

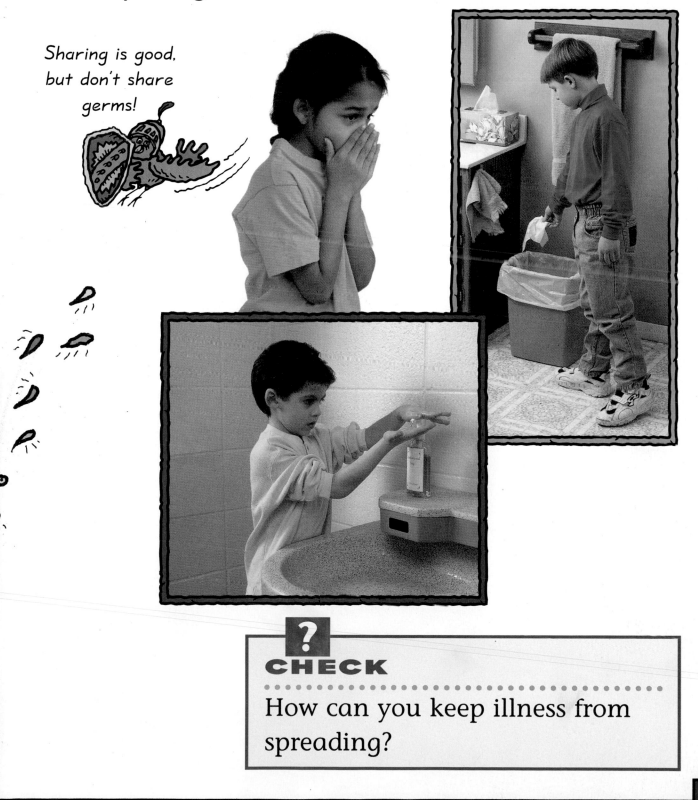

What illness do children often get?

Most children catch colds. Colds are spread by germs. You can watch for the signs of a cold.

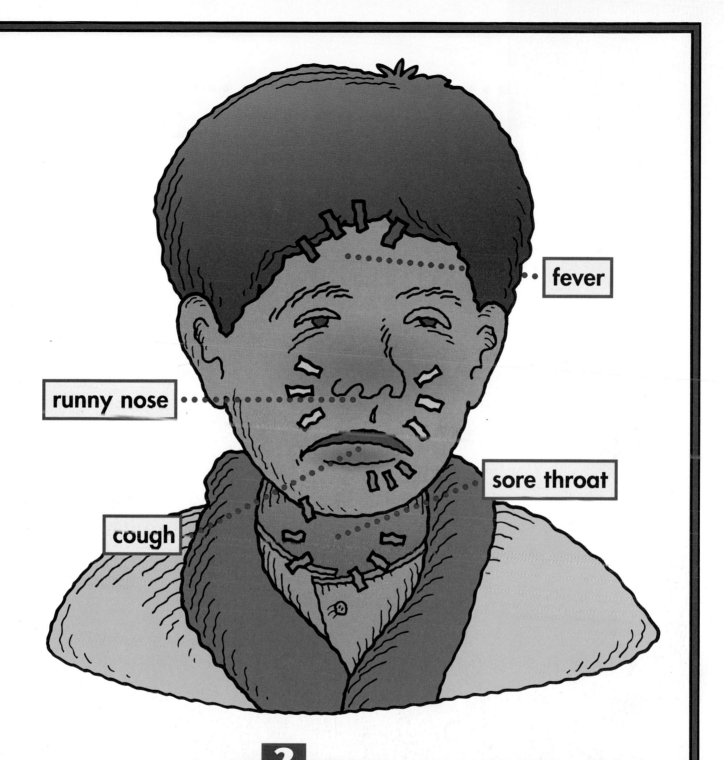

fever

runny nose

sore throat

cough

? CHECK

Point to the parts of your body where you would find the signs of a cold.

How can we stop some diseases?

Vaccines can keep you from getting some diseases. Most children start getting vaccines when they are babies.

Vaccines
help keep you
healthy.

Vaccines can keep you from getting measles, mumps, and chicken pox. Vaccines protect your body. They keep you healthy.

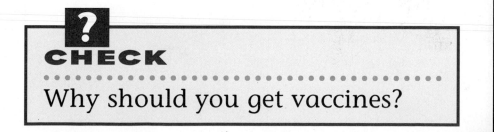

? CHECK

Why should you get vaccines?

What makes me sneeze when I am not ill?

You might have an allergy if you sneeze when you do not have a cold. An **allergy** is an unhealthy way your body reacts to something around you.

An allergy can make you have a rash. An allergy can make your eyes and nose itch. An allergy can make it hard for you to breathe.

Different things cause allergies in different people. Some people have no allergies. Some people have many allergies. There are ways to feel better if you have allergies.

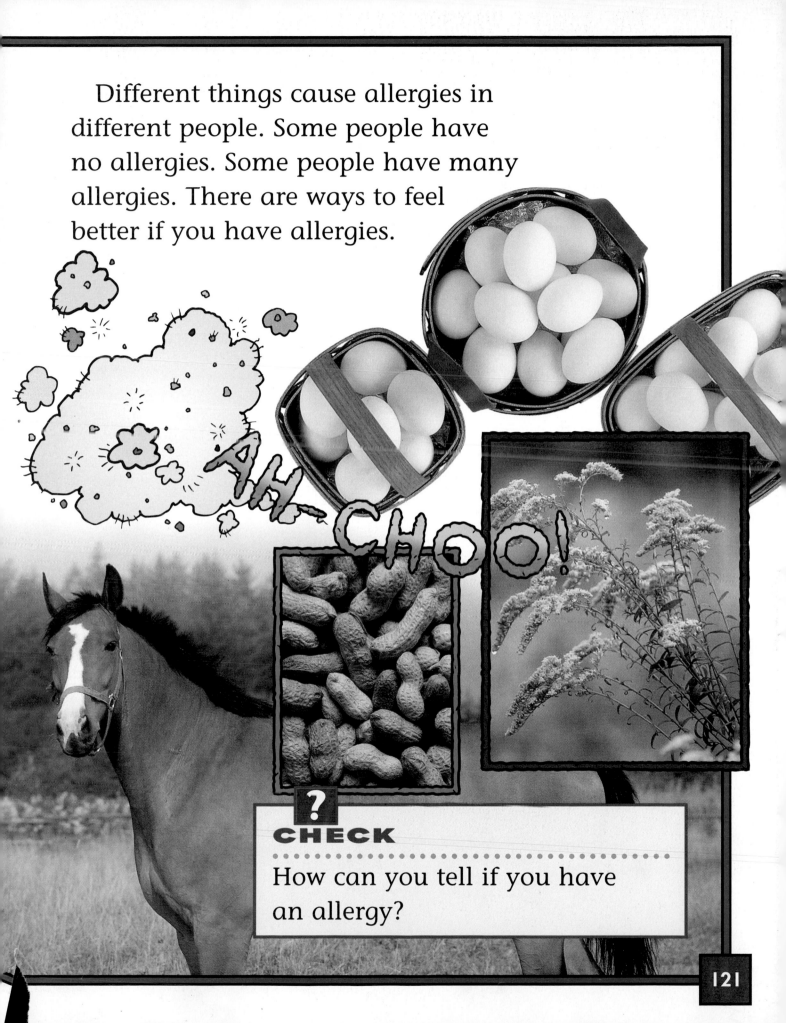

AH-CHOO!

? **CHECK**

How can you tell if you have an allergy?

How can I stay well?

You can do many things that will help you stay well. Look at the pictures. What are these children doing?

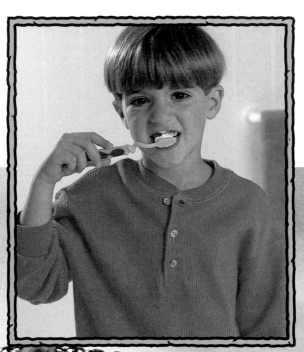

There is one more thing you can do to stay well. You can have fun!

? CHECK

Why do you think having fun can help you stay well?

Review

Use Health Words

| ill | disease | communicate |
| vaccines | allergy | |

Finish the sentences.

1. If you sneeze when you are not ill, you may have an ___.

2. Another word for illness spread by germs is ___.

3. People get ___ to keep them from getting diseases.

4. If your body hurts and you have a fever, you are ___.

5. When you are ill you should ___, or tell someone how you feel.

Use Health Ideas

Answer the questions.

6. Tell how illness is spread.

7. What are the signs of a cold?

8. Tell what these children are doing to help themselves stay well.

Use Life Skills

Answer the questions.

9. What should you do if you feel ill at school?

10. List four steps that will help you communicate when you are ill.

Activities

- **On Your Own** Make a poster that shows one way to help yourself stay well.

- **With a Partner** Make up a puppet show about how to keep germs from spreading.

About Medicines and Drugs

Project

No Drugs!
Make a poster
or sticker to
remind you to
say no to drugs.

**For more things to do,
visit the Internet.
http://www.hbschool.com**

What are medicines used for?

People take **medicines** to feel better. Some medicines help people who are ill get well. Some medicines keep people from getting ill.

Be careful! Medicines can look or taste like candy. Never take medicines when you're not ill.

Medicines can be liquids.
They can be powders.
Medicines can be creams.
They can be pills.

When should people take
medicines?

How can people use medicines safely?

Medicines are **drugs**. When children take medicines, they need help from adults. Doctors and nurses can give medicines. Parents and other adult family members can give medicines.

Cough
Relief

Quiets Coughs
Clears Stuffy N

Never take medicines by yourself. Never play with medicines. Safety caps help keep medicines away from children.

Families can follow rules for using medicines safely. Read the labels carefully. Keep all medicines locked up.

?
CHECK
Who could help you if you needed to take medicines?

What are common drugs?

Some drugs are not medicines. They are common drugs. They can hurt the body.

Caffeine is a common drug. It is in coffee, tea, and soft drinks. Caffeine is also in chocolate.

There are common drugs in **tobacco**. Tobacco is used to make cigarettes and cigars. Some people smoke tobacco in pipes. Some people chew tobacco.

Alcohol is a common drug. It is in beer and wine. Alcohol is in some other drinks, too.

Some drugs are **legal**. They are allowed by the law. Caffeine is legal for everyone. Tobacco and alcohol are legal for adults. Tobacco and alcohol are not legal for children.

? CHECK

How are caffeine, tobacco, and alcohol different from medicines?

What does caffeine do to the body?

Caffeine is a drug. Drugs change the way the body works.

Too much caffeine is not good. It makes the heart beat fast. Too much caffeine can keep some people from falling asleep.

Children should not have too much caffeine. Choose foods and drinks that don't have caffeine.

?
CHECK
....
Which foods in the picture above have caffeine? Which do not?

What does tobacco do to the body?

There are drugs in tobacco. There are drugs in tobacco smoke. **Tobacco smoke** comes from cigarettes, cigars, and pipes.

The drugs in tobacco speed the body up. They make the heart beat faster. Tobacco can cause lung disease. Tobacco can cause cancer.

A **habit** is something people do over and over. Using tobacco is a bad habit. It is a habit that hurts people.

JOIN THE GREAT AMERICAN SMOKEOUT

10th Anniversary

MAKE THIS YOUR YEAR! TAKE A DAY OFF FROM SMOKING NOV. 20

AMERICAN CANCER SOCIETY

Just for the health of it!

Just for the health of it!

? CHECK

How do the drugs in tobacco and tobacco smoke hurt the body?

What does alcohol do to the body?

Alcohol is a drug. When people drink alcohol, it goes to the brain. It slows down some parts of the body and speeds up other parts. Drinking too much alcohol can stop a person's heart or breathing.

Drinking alcohol is not legal for children. Alcohol is not healthful for any child.

? CHECK

Name two things drinking alcohol can do to the body.

How can I stay away from drugs?

You can refuse drugs. To **refuse** means to say no to something.

You can take medicines when an adult in your family gives them to you. You can also take medicines from a nurse or a doctor. Refuse to take medicines from anyone else.

Do not drink alcohol. Do not touch glasses, cans, or bottles that hold alcohol.

Do not touch tobacco packages. Stay away from tobacco smoke.

? **CHECK**
....

Why should you stay away from drugs?

SAY NO to Drugs

Tanya is at her friend Nancy's house. She keeps sneezing and coughing. Nancy offers Tanya some of her cold medicine. No adult is around. How can Tanya refuse?

Learn This Skill

1. Say no, and tell why.

2. Think about what could happen.

I'm not supposed to take other people's medicine.

Tanya says no to Nancy. She tells Nancy why she is refusing.

It could make me ill.

Tanya knows that medicines should not be shared.

3. Suggest something else to do.

I'll call my mom and ask what I should do.

Tanya decides to ask her mom what to do.

4. Repeat no, and walk away.

My mom says I don't have a cold, so I don't need medicine. I'm allergic to your cat! Let's go play at my house.

Tanya finds out that she was right to refuse the medicine.

Practice This Skill

Use the steps to help you solve the problem below.

Jimmy plays roller hockey with some older boys. One of them offers Jimmy some chewing tobacco. How can Jimmy refuse?

Use Health Words

medicines **drugs** **caffeine**
tobacco **alcohol**

Finish the sentences.

1. Things that change the way the body works are called ___.

2. The drug in coffee and chocolate is ___.

3. Cigarettes are made from ___.

4. When people are ill, they may take ___ to feel better.

5. The common drug in beer and wine is ___.

Use Health Ideas

Answer the questions.

6. Name two ways to use medicines safely.

7. How does tobacco smoke harm the body?

Use the picture to answer the questions.

8. Which things in the picture have caffeine?

9. Which things have alcohol?

Use Life Skills

Answer the question.

10. Someone dares you to drink beer. What do you say? What do you do?

Activities

- **On Your Own** Make a button or sticker to remind yourself to say no to drugs.

- **At Home** Make a list of foods and drinks your family has that contain caffeine.

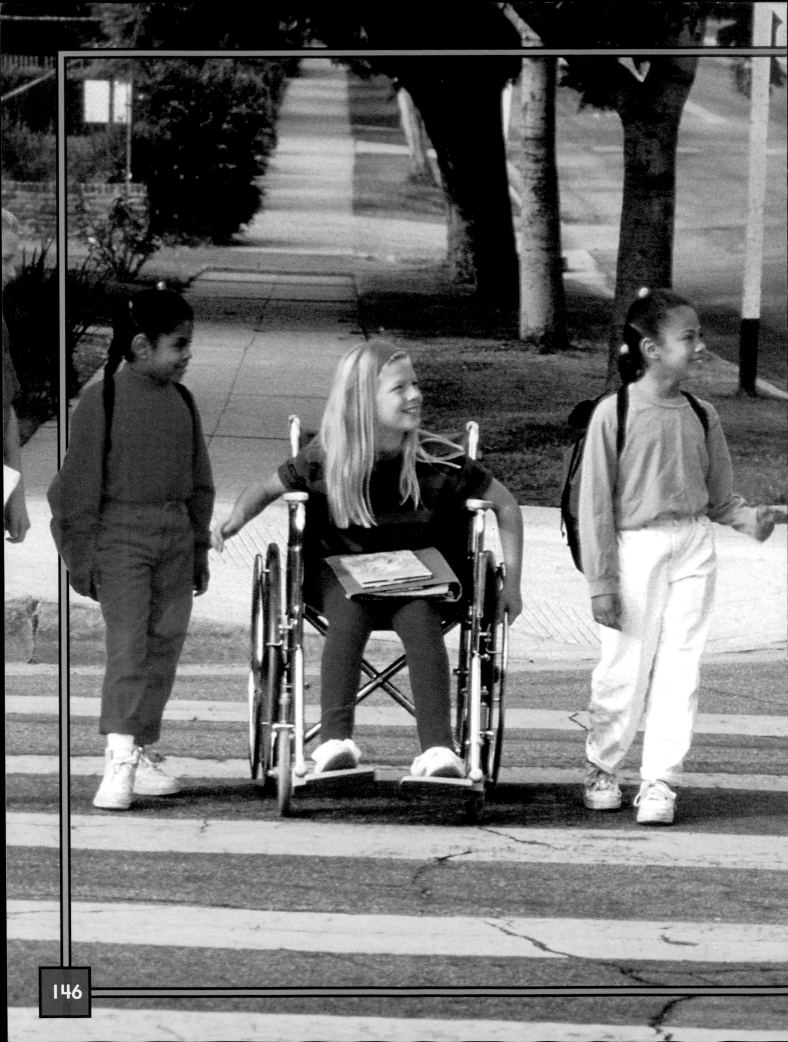

Being Safe

Project

Safety First!

Pretend you are in charge of school safety. Make up five rules that will keep everyone safe at school.

For more things to do, visit the Internet.
http://www.hbschool.com

How can I cross streets safely?

You can stay safe when you cross the street. Always choose a safe place to cross, such as a crosswalk. A **crosswalk** is a marked place to cross a street safely.

Follow the steps to cross safely.

1. Stop.
Do not walk into the street before you stop.

2. Look.

Be sure to look both ways for **traffic**, which is anything moving on a street or highway.

3. Listen.

You might not see any traffic. But if you hear traffic coming, you should not cross.

Vroom...

4. Think.

Pay attention. Keep moving as you cross the street to stay safe.

? CHECK

Act out how to cross the street safely.

How can I stay safe in a car?

You can stay safe when you ride in a car. You should ride in the back seat. Always wear a safety belt. **Safety belts** are straps that hold you safely in your seat. Buckle your safety belt before the car starts moving.

These pictures show how you can stay safe in a car.

Buckle up!

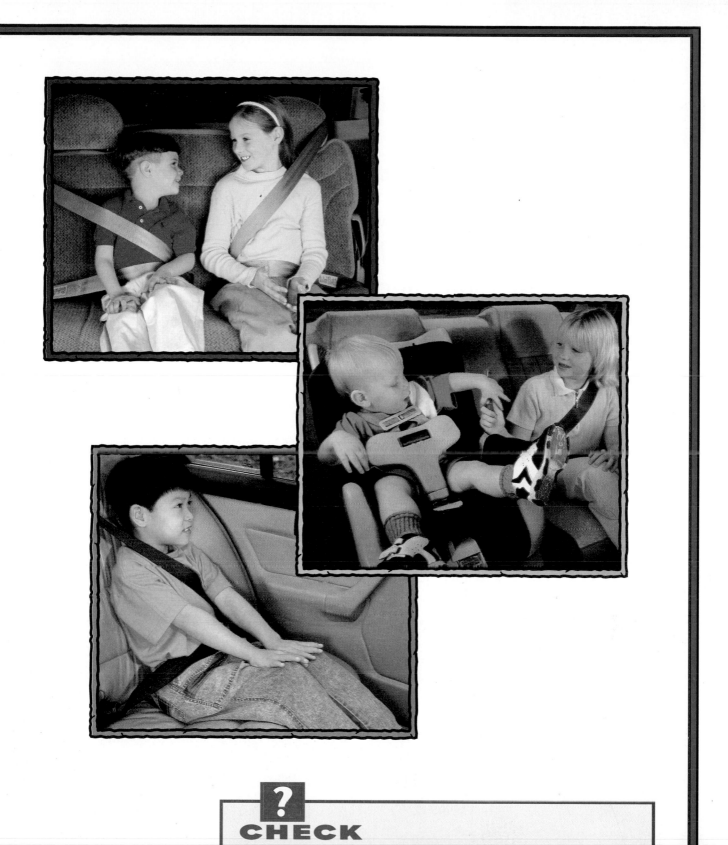

? CHECK

What should you always do before the car starts moving?

How can I stay safe at home?

You can stay safe at home. You can do things to make your home a safe place.

Do you know what to do in an emergency? An **emergency** is a time when help is needed right away. Use the phone to call 911.

Frequently Called Numbers

DAD AT WORK	555-9378
MOM AT WORK	555-2525
GRANDMA	555-1324
DOCTOR	555-0327
SCHOOL	555-1723

In Case of Emergency Call 911

? CHECK

Name three ways to make your home a safe place.

How can I stay safe from fires?

You can stay safe from fires. Do not play with matches or lighters. Matches and lighters are not toys.

Stay away from stoves and heaters. Do not touch electric plugs.

A fire is an emergency. If there is a fire, leave your home. Call 911 from another phone.

Practice the best way to leave your home if there is a fire.

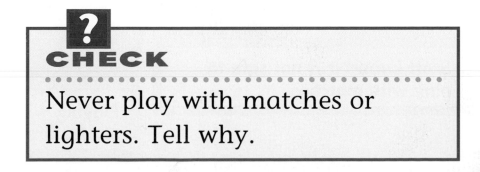

? CHECK

Never play with matches or lighters. Tell why.

SAY NO and Stay Safe

Scott is at Kirk's house. Kirk finds matches and wants to play with them. What should Scott do?

Learn This Skill

1. Name the problem, and say no.

2. Think about what could happen.

No! Matches aren't safe. Don't touch them.

Scott knows it is not safe to play with matches.

We could start a fire.

Playing with matches could start a fire.

3. Suggest something else to do.

Scott wants Kirk to do something different. He suggests a safe way to have fun.

4. Say no again, and walk away.

Scott will not stay at Kirk's house unless Kirk puts the matches away.

Practice This Skill

Use the steps to help you solve this problem.

You are at your friend's house after school. Your friend's mother is next door visiting a neighbor. Your friend wants to cook something to eat. You don't think it is safe to cook without help from an adult.

How can I stay safe at school?

You can stay safe at school. Follow the rules to stay safe in class, in the halls, and on the playground. When you use **playground equipment**, be careful.

Be careful with sharp things.

Walk, don't run, in the halls.

Don't climb on chairs or tables.

Ee Ff Gg Hh Ii Jj Kk Ll Mm Nn Oo Pp

How can I stay safe on the bus?

You can stay safe on the bus. The bus driver will help you. But you have a responsibility to take care of yourself, too. A **responsibility** is something you need to do on your own.

The bus driver has a responsibility to drive safely. Your responsibility is to do what the bus driver tells you.

MAIN STREET APARTMENTS

STOP

68

You have a responsibility to get on and off the bus safely. You have a responsibility to stay in your seat. You have a responsibility to talk quietly. Then the bus driver can pay attention to the road.

? **CHECK**

Name two ways to stay safe when you are getting on or off the bus.

7

How can I stay safe around strangers?

When you are away from home or school, strangers are around. A **stranger** is someone you do not know.

You must be careful around strangers. You could be in danger. You are in **danger** when something may harm you.

You can stay safe around strangers. Follow the rules.

- Never go anywhere with a stranger.

- Never take anything from a stranger.

- Don't talk to strangers.

- If you are lost or you need help, ask a police officer, a guard, or a store clerk.

Tri-State Mall
Lost and Found
Please
See security for assistance
Thank You

?
CHECK
Pretend a stranger asks you to go for a ride. Act out what you would do.

163

Review

Use Health Words

safety belts   emergency

responsibility   stranger

Finish the sentences.

1. Someone you do not know is a ___.

2. The bus driver has a ___ to help you ride safely.

3. You should call 911 if there is an ___.

4. All the people in a car must wear ___.

Use Health Ideas

Answer the questions.

5. List four rules for crossing the street safely.

6. Name two ways to stay safe from fires.

7. What should you do if a stranger offers you a ride?

Tell what is missing in each picture that would help keep the boy safe.

8. **9.** **10.**

Use Life Skills

Use what you know about saying no to solve this problem.

11. Your friend wants to take a short cut to the park. He wants to run across the highway. What do you say?

Activities

- **On Your Own** Draw a map that shows the safest way to walk to school or a neighbor's house.

- **At Home** Make a fire safety plan with your family.

Keeping My Neighborhood Healthy

Project

A Map to Health
Make a map of your community. Show where people work to make your neighborhood healthy and safe.

For more things to do, visit the Internet.
http://www.hbschool.com

Who keeps the community healthy?

Your **community** is the place where you live. Many people work to make your community healthy and safe.

Look at the pictures. How are these people helping?

DANGER
BEACH
CLOSED

?

CHECK

How do community workers help you?

What do nurses do?

A **nurse** is someone who helps people who are hurt or ill. Nurses work in many places.

A nurse may work in a **clinic**. A clinic is a place where sick people can get help.

Some nurses visit sick people at home.

You may see a nurse at school.
A school nurse helps children who
become ill or get hurt at school.
A school nurse also helps children
stay healthy.

? CHECK
....
How can a nurse help you?

3

What do doctors do?

A **doctor** is someone who helps people who are ill or hurt. Doctors can find out what is wrong. They can tell what to do. Doctors know ways to keep people from getting sick.

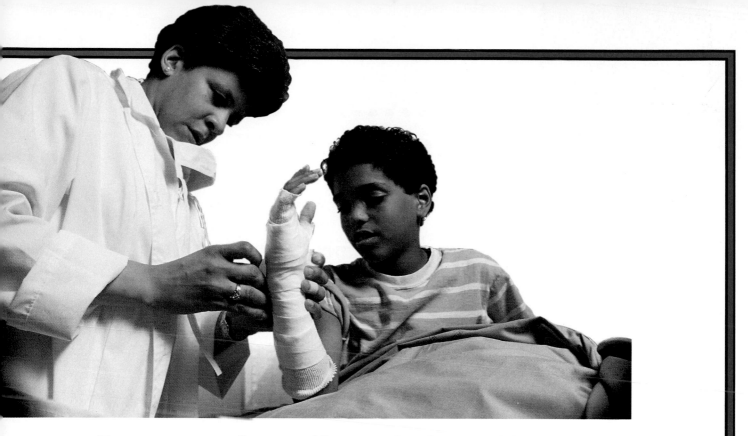

Doctors work in offices, clinics, and hospitals. Some doctors take care of your whole body. Some doctors take care of only one part of your body.

? CHECK

Name two times when you would need a doctor's help.

Who keeps a neighborhood clean?

Your **environment** is everything around you. You want your environment to be clean and safe.

Garbage has germs in it. Germs can make you sick. Nobody wants garbage to pile up everywhere.

Community workers help keep your neighborhood clean and safe. They clean up garbage.

? CHECK

Who helps keep your neighborhood clean and safe?

What can make less trash?

Trash makes a neighborhood dirty. Trash is what you throw away. You can help keep your neighborhood clean and safe. Put your trash in trash cans. Trash that is not thrown away properly is called **litter**.

Don't be a litterbug!

You can make less trash. Use things more than once. Don't waste paper. Share with a friend.

?
CHECK
Tell where you should put trash at home and at school.

177

MAKE DECISIONS
About Trash

You can help make less trash. Make a choice to reuse things instead of throwing them away.

Kenny's family has a lot of empty boxes. How can Kenny help his family decide what to do with them?

Learn This Skill

1. Think before you choose.

2. Imagine what could happen with each choice.

Let's just throw them in the trash.

What should we do with these?

Let's use them some other way.

Kenny's family has a lot of boxes left over from moving.

The family members think about their choices.

3. Make the best choice.

4. Think about what happened.

OK. We can make files for our sports magazines.

I think we should reuse them so we have less trash.

Kenny's choice helps the family reuse the boxes.

Now Kenny's family has less trash.

Practice This Skill

Use the steps to help you solve this problem.

Nina has to make a costume for a school play. She can buy new materials. Or she can use some old materials her sister is going to throw away. What should Nina do?

What can be made from trash?

You make less trash when you recycle. You **recycle** something when you use it over and over. Think before you throw something away. Maybe you can find another way to use it.

CONTA
NON-CA
CONTA
corn sy
citric a

NESTLÉ
345 SPEA
SAN FRA
CA 9410

Look at the picture. How many recycled things can you find?

? **CHECK**

Why should you recycle things?

Review

CHAPTER 9

Use Health Words

community	nurse	clinic
doctor	environment	litter
recycle		

Finish the sentences.

1. Your ___ is everything around you.

2. The place where you live is your ___.

3. Some people who are ill have a ___ visit them at home.

4. If you are hurt or ill, a ___ can find out what is wrong and help you get better.

5. When you use something over and over, you ___ it.

6. One place you can get help if you are ill is a ___.

7. Trash that is not thrown away properly is ___.

Use Health Ideas

Tell how each of these workers helps keep your community healthy and safe.

8.  9.  10.

Answer the question.

11. Why should people try to make less garbage and trash?

Use Life Skills

Use what you know about making decisions to answer the question.

12. Which picture shows the best choice about trash? Explain your answer.

Activities

- **On Your Own** Think of a way to reuse something you might throw away at school.

- **With a Partner** Act out a visit to the school nurse.

1 Say no!

2 Get away.

NO!

Getting Exercise

❸ Tell someone.

Staying Safe

Bike Safety

Warm-Up and Cool-Down Stretches

▼ **Shoulder and Chest Stretch** Pull your hands slowly toward the floor. Keep your elbows straight, but don't lock them.

Warm up your muscles before you exercise. Spend at least five minutes stretching. You can use any of the stretches shown here. Hold each stretch while you count to 15. Repeat each stretch three times. Remember to start exercising slowly.

Slow down at the end of exercise. Then repeat some of these stretches for about two minutes. Stretching after exercise helps your muscles cool down.

▶ **Sit-and-Reach Stretch** Bend forward at the waist. Keep your eyes on your toes.

◀ **Calf Stretch** Keep both feet on the floor. Try changing the distance between your feet. Where do you get a better stretch?

186

▲ **Upper Back and Shoulder Stretch**
Try to stretch your hand down so
that it rests flat against your back.

▼ **Thigh Stretch** Keep both hands
flat on the ground. Lean as far
forward as you can.

▲ **Leg Stretch**
Extend one leg
behind you.
Keep the toes
of that foot
pointed up.

Tips for Stretching

- Never bounce. Stretch gently.
- Breathe normally to get the air you need.
- Never stretch until it hurts. You should
  feel only a slight pull.

187

Build Your Heart and Lungs

Exercise helps your heart and lungs grow strong. The best exercise activities make you breathe deeply. They make your heart beat fast. You should try to exercise for at least twenty minutes at a time. Remember to warm up first and cool down at the end.

▲ **Swimming** If you are not a strong swimmer, use a kickboard to get a good workout. Remember to swim only when a lifeguard is present.

◄ **Skating** Always wear a helmet, elbow and knee pads, wrist guards, and gloves. Learn to skate, stop, and fall correctly.

▼ **Riding a Bike** When you ride your bike, your exercise really gets you somewhere! Follow bike safety rules, and always wear your helmet.

▶ **Walking** A fast walk can help build your heart and lungs. Wear shoes that support your feet. Walk with a friend for extra fun!

▶ **Jumping Rope** Jumping rope is good for your heart and your lungs. Always jump on a flat surface. Wear shoes that support your feet.

189

The President's Challenge

The President's Challenge is a physical fitness program for children ages six to seventeen. There are five activities in the President's Challenge. Each activity tests the fitness of a different part of your body. Your teacher can tell you more about how to take the President's Challenge.

❶ Curl-Ups or Sit-Ups

This exercise measures strength in the muscles below your stomach.

❷ Shuttle Run

This exercise measures the strength of your legs. It also tests your heart and lungs.

❸ One Mile Run or Walk

This exercise measures the strength of your legs. It tests how long you can exercise without getting tired.

❹ Pull-Ups

This exercise measures strength in the muscles of your arms and shoulders.

❺ V-Sit Reach

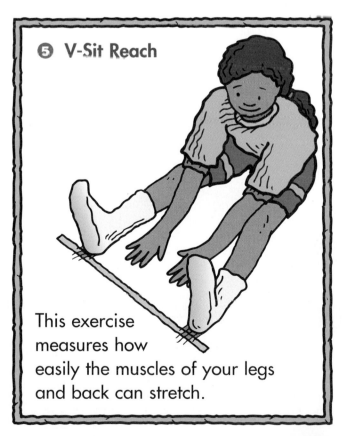

This exercise measures how easily the muscles of your legs and back can stretch.

Fire Safety

You can stay safe from fires. Follow these safety rules.

- Never play with matches or lighters.
- Be careful around stoves, heaters, fireplaces, and grills.
- Don't use microwaves, irons, or toasters without an adult's help.
- Practice your family's fire safety plan.
- If there is a fire in your home, get out quickly. Drop to the floor and crawl if the room is filled with smoke. If a closed door feels hot, don't open it. Use another exit. Call 911 from outside your home.
- If your clothes catch on fire, use Stop, Drop, and Roll right away to put out the flames.

❶ **Stop** Don't run or wave your arms.

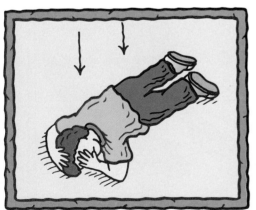

❷ **Drop** Lie down quickly. Cover your eyes with your hands.

❸ **Roll** Roll back and forth to put out the fire.

Stranger Danger

You can stay safe around strangers. Follow these rules.

- Never talk to strangers.
- Never go with a stranger, on foot or in a car.
- If you are home alone, do not open the door. Do not let telephone callers know you are alone.
- Never give your name, address, or phone number to anyone you don't know. (You may give this information to a 911 operator in an emergency.)
- If you are lost or need help, talk to a police officer, a guard, or a store clerk.
- If a stranger bothers you, use the Stranger Danger rules to stay safe.

❶ **Say no!** Yell if you need to. You do not have to be polite to strangers.

❷ **Get away.** Walk fast or run in the opposite direction. Go toward people who can help you.

❸ **Tell someone.** Tell a trusted adult, such as a family member, a teacher, or a police officer. Do not keep secrets about strangers.

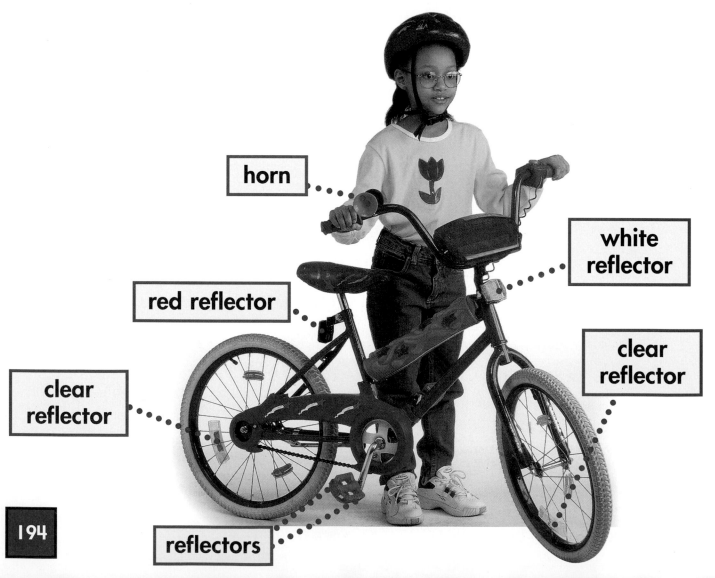

A Safe Bike

To ride your bike safely, you need to start with a safe bike. A safe bike is the right size for you. When you sit on your bike with the pedal in the lowest position, you should be able to rest your heel on the pedal.

After checking the size of your bike, check to see that it has the right safety equipment. Your bike should have everything shown below.

horn

white reflector

red reflector

clear reflector

clear reflector

reflectors

Your Bike Helmet

◄ **Always wear a bike helmet. Wear your helmet flat on your head. Be sure it is strapped tightly. If your helmet gets bumped in a fall, replace it right away, even if it doesn't look damaged.**

Safety on the Road

- Check your bike for safety every time you ride it.
- Ride in single file. Ride in the same direction as traffic.
- Stop, look, listen, and think when you enter a street or cross a driveway.
- Walk your bike across an intersection.
- Obey all traffic signs and signals.
- Don't ride at night without an adult. Wear light-colored clothing and use lights and reflectors for night riding.

Glossary

ad (AD): a message that tries to get you to buy something (104)

alcohol (AL•kuh•hawl): the drug found in beer, wine, and liquor (132)

allergy (A•luhr•jee): an unhealthy way your body reacts to something around you (120)

angry (AN•gree): feeling upset at someone or about something (22)

arm bones (ARM BOHNZ): the bones of the arms (4)

arm muscles (ARM MUH•suhlz): the muscles that allow the arms to move (12)

blood vessels (BLUHD VEH•suhlz): the tubes of the circulatory system that carry blood through the body (8)

brain (BRAYN): the part of the nervous system that directs the way the body works (13)

breakfast (BREK•fuhst): the first and most important meal of the day (98)

caffeine (ka•FEEN): the drug found in coffee, tea, chocolate, and some soft drinks (132)

circulatory system (SER•kyuh•luh•tohr•ee SIS•tuhm): the parts of the body that work together to carry blood through the body (8)

clinic (KLIH•nik): a place where people who are ill or hurt can get help (170)

communicate (kuh•MYOO•nuh•kayt): talk to and listen to someone else (112)

community (kuh•MYOO•nuh•tee): the place where you live (168)

conflict (KAWN•flikt): a disagreement or an argument between people (46)

crosswalk (KRAWS•wawk): a marked place to safely cross a street (148)

danger (DAYN•jer): something bad that could happen (162)

dental hygienist (DEN•tuhl hy•JEE•nist): a person who helps clean and take care of your teeth (67)

dentists (DEN•tuhsts): doctors who take care of teeth (66)

digestive system (dy•JES•tiv SIS•tuhm): the parts of your body that work together to help you get energy from food (6)

dinner (DIH•ner): the meal most people eat in the evening (98)

disease (dih•ZEEZ): illness spread by germs (114)

doctor (DAWK•ter): someone who helps people who are ill or hurt by finding out what is wrong and telling what to do to get well (172)

drugs (DRUHGZ): things that change the way the body works (130)

eardrum (IR•druhm): the thin piece of tissue in the ear that helps you hear (3)

emergency (ih•MER•juhnt•see): a time when help is needed right away; a time to call 911 (153)

energy (EH•ner•jee): the power your body needs to do things (90)

environment (in•VY•ruhn•muhnt): everything around you (174)

exercise (EK•ser•syz): active use of your body (78)

face muscles (FAYS MUH•suhlz): the muscles that help you smile and frown (12)

family (FAM•lee): people such as a mom, a stepdad, a brother, or an aunt (42)

feelings (FEE•lingz): what you feel inside when you are happy, sad, afraid, or excited (18)

floss (FLAWS): a special thread used to clean the teeth (60)

Food Guide Pyramid (FOOD GYD PIR•uh•mid): a diagram that shows people which foods to eat, and how much of them to eat, to stay healthy (93)

friends (FRENDZ): people you enjoy being with who are not family members (28)

germs (JERMZ): tiny things that carry disease and can make you ill (72)

growing (GROH•ing): becoming bigger, taller, and older (41)

habit (HA•bit): something people do over and over (137)

heart (HART): the muscle of the circulatory system that pumps blood through the body (8)

hip bones (HIP BOHNZ): the bones of the hips (4)

ill (IL): not well or healthy (110)

inner ear (IH•ner IR): the part of the ear deepest in the head, behind the eardrum (3)

iris (EYE•ruhs): the colored part of the eye (2)

leg bones (LEG BOHNZ): the bones of the legs (4)

leg muscles (LEG MUH•suhlz): the muscles that allow the legs to move (12)

legal (LEE•guhl): allowed by the law (133)

litter (LIH•ter): trash that is not thrown away properly (176)

living (LIH•ving): things that are alive (34)

love (LUHV): a special feeling of caring you have for your family and good friends (43)

lunch (LUHNCH): the meal most people eat in the middle of the day (98)

lungs (LUHNGZ): the parts of the respiratory system that pump air in and out of the body (10)

medicines (MEH•duh•suhnz): drugs that can help people get well or stay healthy (128)

middle ear (MIH•duhl IR): the part of the ear just inside the head, separated from the inner ear by the eardrum (3)

mouth (MOWTH): the part of the digestive system that takes in food (6); a part of the respiratory system that takes in and lets out air (10)

muscular system (MUHS•kyuh•ler SIS•tuhm): the parts of the body that work together to allow movement (12)

neck muscles (NEK MUH•suhlz): the muscles used to support and turn the head (12)

nerves (NERVZ): parts of the body that carry messages to and from the brain (13)

nervous system (NER•vuhs SIS•tuhm): the parts of the body that work together to carry messages to and from the brain and to help you feel things (13)

nonliving (NAWN•LIH•ving): things that are not alive (35)

nose (NOHZ): a part of the respiratory system that takes in and lets out air; the part of your body that uses the sense of smell (10)

nurse (NERS): someone who helps people who are ill or hurt (170)

permanent teeth (PER•muh•nuhnt TEETH): your second set of teeth, which you get after your primary teeth fall out (57)

playground equipment (PLAY•grownd ih•KWIP•muhnt): swings, slides, climbing bars, and other things on a playground (158)

polite (puh•LYT): showing respect and treating others nicely (44)

posture (PAWS•cher): the way you hold your body when you stand, sit, or move (76)

primary teeth (PRY•mair•ee TEETH): your baby teeth, the first set of teeth you get (56)

pupil (PYOO•puhl): the hole in the center of the eye that opens and closes to let in light (2)

recycle (ree•SY•kuhl): using the materials in something over and over (180)

refuse (rih•FYOOZ): to say no to someone or something (140)

respect (rih•SPEKT): treating others nicely (26)

respiratory system (RES•puh•ruh•tohr•ee SIS•tuhm): the parts of the body that work together to help you breathe (10)

responsibility (rih•spahnt•suh•BIH•luh•tee): something you need to do on your own (160)

safety belts (SAYF•tee BELTZ): straps that hold you safely in your seat in a car, truck, van, or airplane (150)

senses (SEN•suhz): ways you use your body to learn, enjoy things, and stay safe; sight, hearing, smell, taste, and touch (36)

skeletal system (SKEH•luh•tuhl SIS•tuhm): the bones; the parts of the body that support and protect softer parts (4)

skeleton (SKEH•luh•tuhn): all the bones of the body shown together (4)

skull (SKUHL): the bones of the head (5)

snack (SNAK): food you eat to give you energy between meals (102)

special (SPEH•shuhl): different from everyone else (16)

spine (SPYN): the bones of the back and neck (5)

stomach (STUH•muhk): the part of the digestive system where food is broken down (6)

stomach muscles (STUH•muhk MUH•suhlz): the muscles of the stomach area (12)

stranger (STRAYN•jer): someone you do not know (162)

stress (STRES): a way the body reacts to strong feelings (24)

stretch (STRECH): gently pulling your muscles as a way to warm up before exercise and cool down after exercise (82)

sunburn (SUHN•bern): a burning of the skin caused by the sun's rays (74)

sunscreen (SUHN•skreen): a lotion or cream that keeps the sun's rays from burning your skin (75)

teeth (TEETH): the parts of the digestive system used to bite and chew food (7)

tobacco (tuh•BA•koh): material made from dried plant leaves that contains drugs and is smoked or chewed in cigarettes, cigars, pipes, and chewing tobacco (132)

tobacco smoke (tuh•BA•koh SMOHK): smoke from tobacco, which contains drugs and is harmful to people who breathe it (136)

tongue (TUHNG): the part of the digestive system that helps you taste and swallow food (7)

traffic (TRA•fik): anything moving on a street or highway (149)

vaccines (vak•SEENZ): shots or pills that can keep people from getting some diseases (118)

Boldfaced numbers refer to illustrations.

manage stress with exercise, 80–81, **80–81**

managing feelings, 18–22

planning healthful habits, 69

refuse alcohol, 139

refuse drugs, **126–127,** 140–141, **140–141,** 142–143, **142–143**

refuse tobacco, 137, 141

refusing, 142–143, **142–143,** 156–157, **156–157**

resolve conflicts in the family, 46–47, **46–47**

resolve conflicts with friends, 165

respecting others, 26–27

responding to anger, 22–23, **22–23**

responsibility, 160–161, **160–161**

staying safe, 156–157, **156–157**

Litter, **169,** 176, **176**

Living things, 32–34, **32–34**

Love, **43**

Lunch, choosing healthful, 98–99, **98–99**

Lungs, 10–11, **10–11,** 188

effects of tobacco on, 136, **136**

exercising to build, 78–79, **78–79**

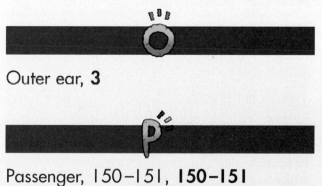

Make decisions

about food, 92–93, 96–97, 100–101, 102

about tooth care, 64–65, **64–65**

about trash, 178–179, **178–179**

Manage stress, 22–23, 24–25, 30

through exercise, 80–81, **81**

Meals, healthful, 98, **98**

Measles, 119

Meat, poultry, fish, dried beans, eggs, and nuts food group, **93,** 95

Medicines

defined, 128–129, **128–129**

safety with, 130–131, **130–131,** 140, 143

Middle ear, **3**

Milk, yogurt, and cheese food group, **92, 95**

Mouth, 6–7, **6–7,** 10–11, **10–11**

Mumps, 119

Muscular system

caring for, 12, 82, **82,** 84, 186–187, **186–187**

exercise for health, **78–79,** 78–79

growth, 41

parts of, 12, **12**

Neck muscles, 12, **12**

Neighborhood, **166–167**

cleanliness of, 174–175, **174–175**

Nerves, 13, **13**

Nervous system

caring for, 13

effects of alcohol on, 138, **138**

effects of caffeine on, 134, **134**

parts of, 13, **13**

911, 153, **153,** 155

Nonliving, 35, **35,** 50

Nose, 10–11, **10–11,** 114, 120

Nurse, 170–171, **170–171**

Outer ear, **3**

Passenger, 150–151, **150–151**

Permanent teeth, **53,** 57, **57**

Playground equipment, 158–159, **159**

Police, 163, **163, 169**

CREDITS

Cover Design: MKR Design, Inc./Robert B. Allen.

Key: (bkgd) background, (tl) top left, (tc) top center, (tr) top right, (c) center, (bl) bottom left, (bc) bottom center, (br) bottom right.

PHOTOGRAPHS:

Cover: Michael Groen.

Body Atlas: 1(bl), Digital Imaging Group; (bc), Digital Imaging Group; (br), Eric Camden Photography.

Chapter 1: 14–15, David R. Frazier Photo Library; 16, Jim Whitmer; 17(tl), Eric Camden Photography; (tr), Michael Newman/PhotoEdit; (br), Alan Hicks/Tony Stone Images; 18, Digital Imaging Group; 19(l), Eric Camden Photography; (r), Digital Imaging Group; 22(l), Digital Imaging Group; (r), Digital Imaging Group; 23(t), Digital Imaging Group; (c), Digital Imaging Group; (b), Digital Imaging Group; 24(l), Digital Imaging Group; (r), Digital Imaging Group; 25(l), Digital Imaging Group; (r), Digital Imaging Group; 26, Jim Whitmer; 27, Digital Imaging Group; 28, Digital Imaging Group; 31, Digital Imaging Group;

Chapter 2: 32–33, Eric Camden Photography; 36, Digital Imaging Group; 37, Jean Higgins/Unicorn Stock; 38(l), Tony Freeman/PhotoEdit; (r), Myrleen Ferguson Cate/PhotoEdit; 39(tl), Peter Krinninger/International Stock; (c), Digital Imaging Group; (bl), Digital Imaging Group; 40(l), Jim Erikson/The Stock Market; (c), J. Pinderhughes/The Stock Market; (r), Richard Gross/The Stock Market; 41(c), Arthur Tilley/FPG International; 42(bl), Chuck Savage/The Stock Market; 42–43(br), Eric Camden Photography; 43(bc), Eric Camden Photography; 44, Myrleen Ferguson Cate/PhotoEdit; 45(tc), Telegraph Colour Library/FPG International; (br), James Davis/International Stock; 46(l), Digital Imaging Group; (r), Digital Imaging Group; 47(l), Digital Imaging Group; (r), Digital Imaging Group; 48, SuperStock; 49(tc), Tony Freeman/PhotoEdit; (c), Jeff Greenberg/David R. Frazier Photo Library; 51(t), Digital Imaging Group; (b), Digital Imaging Group.

Chapter 3: 52–53, Digital Imaging Group; 54, Digital Imaging Group; 56, SuperStock; 57, Jonathan Nourok/PhotoEdit; 60, Digital Imaging Group; 61, Digital Imaging Group; 62, Digital Imaging Group; 64(l), Digital Imaging Group; (r), Digital Imaging Group; 65(l), Digital Imaging Group; (r), Digital Imaging Group; 66, Peter Beck/The Stock Market; 67, Nancy Sheehan/PhotoEdit.

Chapter 4: 70–71, Digital Imaging Group; 72, Digital Imaging Group; 73, Digital Imaging Group; 74, Ed McDonald Photography; 75, Ed McDonald Photography; 76(l), Lawrence Migdale/Tony Stone Images; (r), Digital Imaging Group; 77(t), Digital Imaging Group; (b), Digital Imaging Group; 78, Bill Bachman/PhotoEdit; 79(tl), Mary Kate Denny/PhotoEdit; (tr), Tony Freeman/PhotoEdit; (bl), SuperStock; (br), Lawrence Migdale/Tony Stone Images; 80(l), Ed McDonald Photography; (r), Ed McDonald Photography; 81(l), Ed McDonald Photography; (r), Ed McDonald Photography; 82(l), Digital Imaging Group; (r), Digital Imaging Group; 83, Digital Imaging Group; 85, Digital Imaging Group; 87, Digital Imaging Group.

Chapter 5: 88–89, Digital Imaging Group; 90(bl), Digital Imaging Group; 90–91(bc), Digital Imaging Group; 91(c), David Madison/Tony Stone Images; 94(bl), Jack Holtel; 94–95(br), Jack Holtel; 95(tl), Jack Holtel; (tr), Jack Holtel; (c), Jack Holtel; (bl), Jack Holtel; 96, Digital Imaging Group; 97, Digital Imaging Group; 98, Digital Imaging Group; 99(t), Digital Imaging Group; (b), Digital Imaging Group; 100(l), Digital Imaging Group; (r), Digital Imaging Group; 101(l), Digital Imaging Group; (r), Digital Imaging Group; 102(c), Digital Imaging Group; (bl), Digital Imaging Group; (bc), Digital Imaging Group; (br), Digital Imaging Group; 103(t), Digital Imaging Group; (c), Digital Imaging Group; (b), Jack Holtel; 104, Digital Imaging Group; 107(tl), Digital Imaging Group; (tr), Digital Imaging Group; (br), Digital Imaging Group.

Chapter 6: 108–109, Digital Imaging Group; 110(l), Digital Imaging Group; (r), Digital Imaging Group; 111, Mugshots/The Stock Market; 112(l), Digital Imaging Group; (r), Digital Imaging Group; 113(l), Digital Imaging Group; (r), Digital Imaging Group; 114, Digital Imaging Group; 115(tl), Digital Imaging Group; (tr), Digital Imaging Group; (br), Digital Imaging Group; 116, Digital Imaging Group; 118, Levy/Liaison International; 119, Jose Pelaez Photography/The Stock Market; 120(l), Uniphoto; (r), Eugen Gebhardt/FPG International; 121(tr), Uniphoto; (bl), Uniphoto; (bc), Marco Polo/Phototake; (br), A. Schmidecker/FPG International; 122(tr), Vesey Vanderburg/International Stock; (bc), Susan Lapides/Liaison International; 123(tr), Steven Burr Williams/Liaison International; (c), Dave Carter/The Stock Market; 125(br), Digital Imaging Group.

Chapter 7: 126–127, Eric Camden Photography; 128, Aaron Haupt/David R. Frazier Photo Library; 129(t), Eric Camden Photography; (b), Digital Imaging Group; 130(bl), Digital Imaging Group; 130–131(br), Digital Imaging Group; 131(tr), Digital Imaging Group; 134, Digital Imaging Group; 136–137(c), Jos Palmieri/Uniphoto; 136(bc), Montes De Oca/FPG International; 137, Paul Conklin/PhotoEdit; 139, Eric Camden Photography; 141, Digital Imaging Group; 142(l), Digital Imaging Group; (r), Digital Imaging Group; 143(l), Digital Imaging Group; (r), Digital Imaging Group; 145, Digital Imaging Group.

Chapter 8: 146–147, David Young-Wolff/Tony Stone Images; 150, Eric Camden Photography; 151(tl), Eric Camden Photography; (c), Eric Camden Photography; (bl), Eric Camden Photography; 153, Digital Imaging Group; 155, Ed McDonald Photography; 156(l), Digital Imaging Group; (r), Digital Imaging Group; 157(l), Digital Imaging Group; (r), Digital Imaging Group; 158(l), Digital Imaging Group; (r), Digital Imaging Group; 159(t), Michael Tamborrino/FPG International; (b), Michael Tamborrino/FPG International; 160, Larry Mayer/Liaison International; 161(l), Victoria Bowen Photography; (r), Digital Imaging Group; 162, Kunio Owaki/The Stock Market; 163(l), Digital Imaging Group; (r), Digital Imaging Group; 165, Digital Imaging Group.

Chapter 9: 166–167, Digital Imaging Group; 168(c), Michael Newman/PhotoEdit; (bl), Mark Harmer/FPG International; 168–169(br), David Young-Wolff/PhotoEdit; 169(tc), David Young-Wolff/PhotoEdit; 169(c), Chromosohm/Sohm/Uniphoto; 170–171(c), Digital Imaging Group; 170(bl), Digital Imaging Group; 171, Jim Cummins/FPG International; 172, Index Stock; 173(t), Kate Connell/Liaison International; (b), Michael Keller/The Stock Market; 174, Eric Berndt/Unicorn Stock; 175, Myrleen Ferguson Cate/PhotoEdit; 176–177, Index Stock; 178(l), Digital Imaging Group; (r), Digital Imaging Group; 179(l), Digital Imaging Group; (t), Digital Imaging Group; 180(bc), Michael Litcher/International Stock; 180–181(c), Digital Imaging Group; 181(c), Digital Imaging Group; 183(tr), SuperStock; (c), Tony Freeman/PhotoEdit; (br), Digital Imaging Group.

Handbook: 184(tl), Bill Losh/FPG International; (c), Digital Imaging Group; (bl), Digital Imaging Group; (br), Digital Imaging Group; 185, Digital Imaging Group; 186(tl), Digital Imaging Group; (bl), Digital Imaging Group; (br), Digital Imaging Group; 187(tl), Digital Imaging Group; (tc), Digital Imaging Group; (tr), Digital Imaging Group; (c), Digital Imaging Group; 188(c), Bill Bachman/PhotoEdit; (bl), Bill Losh/FPG International; 189(tl), Eric Camden Photography; (tr), Digital Imaging Group; (bl), Digital Imaging Group; 194(bc), Digital Imaging Group; 195(tl), Digital Imaging Group.

Medical Illustrations: Barbara Cousins/Steven Edsey & Sons.

All Other Illustrations: The Mazer Corporation.

Locations: Blue Ash Elementary School, Blue Ash, OH; City of Blue Ash Fire Department, Blue Ash, OH.

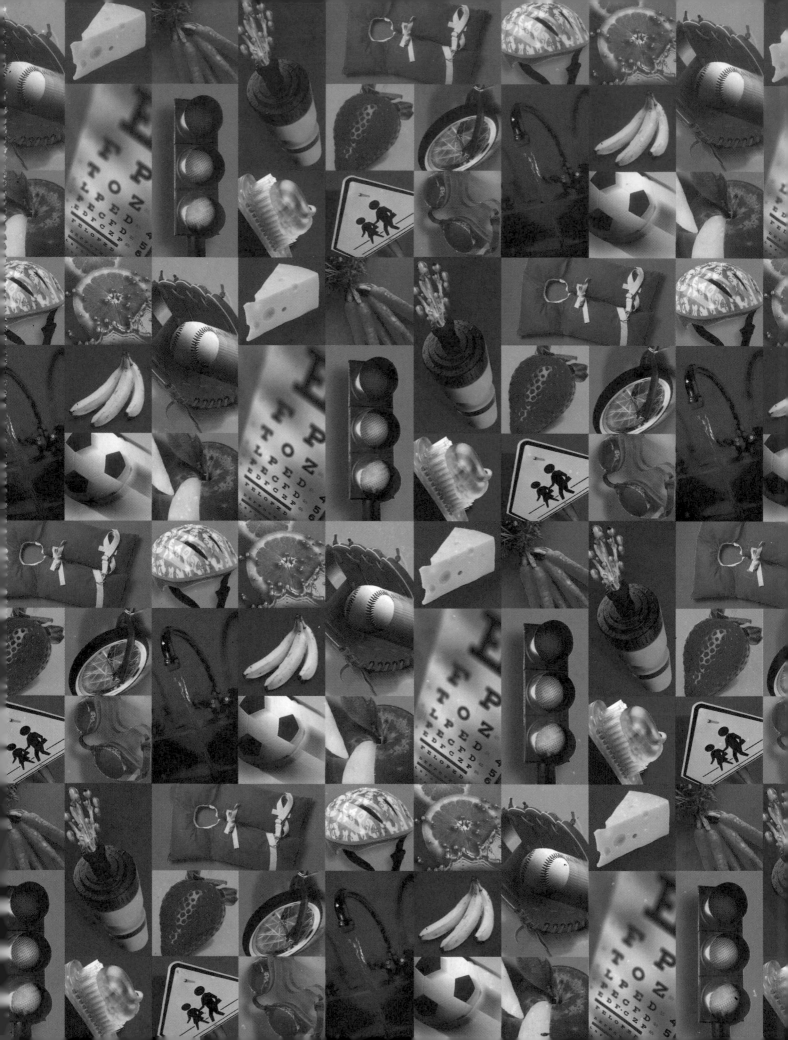